The Cat on the D

By Kaja Foglio with Quinton Hoover and

Once upon a time...

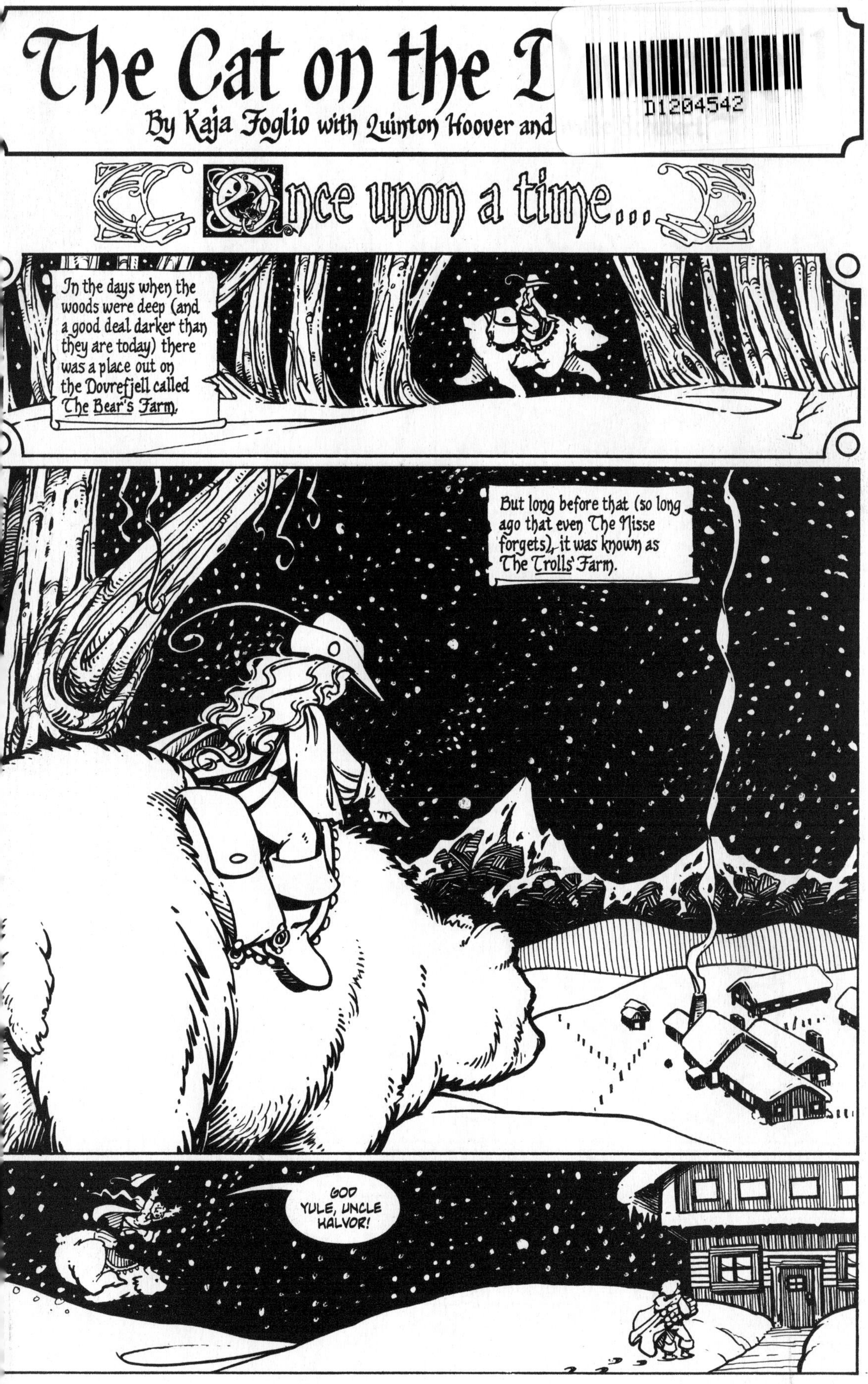
In the days when the woods were deep (and a good deal darker than they are today) there was a place out on the Dovrefjell called The Bear's Farm.
But long before that (so long ago that even The Nisse forgets), it was known as The Trolls' Farm.
GOD YULE, UNCLE HALVOR!

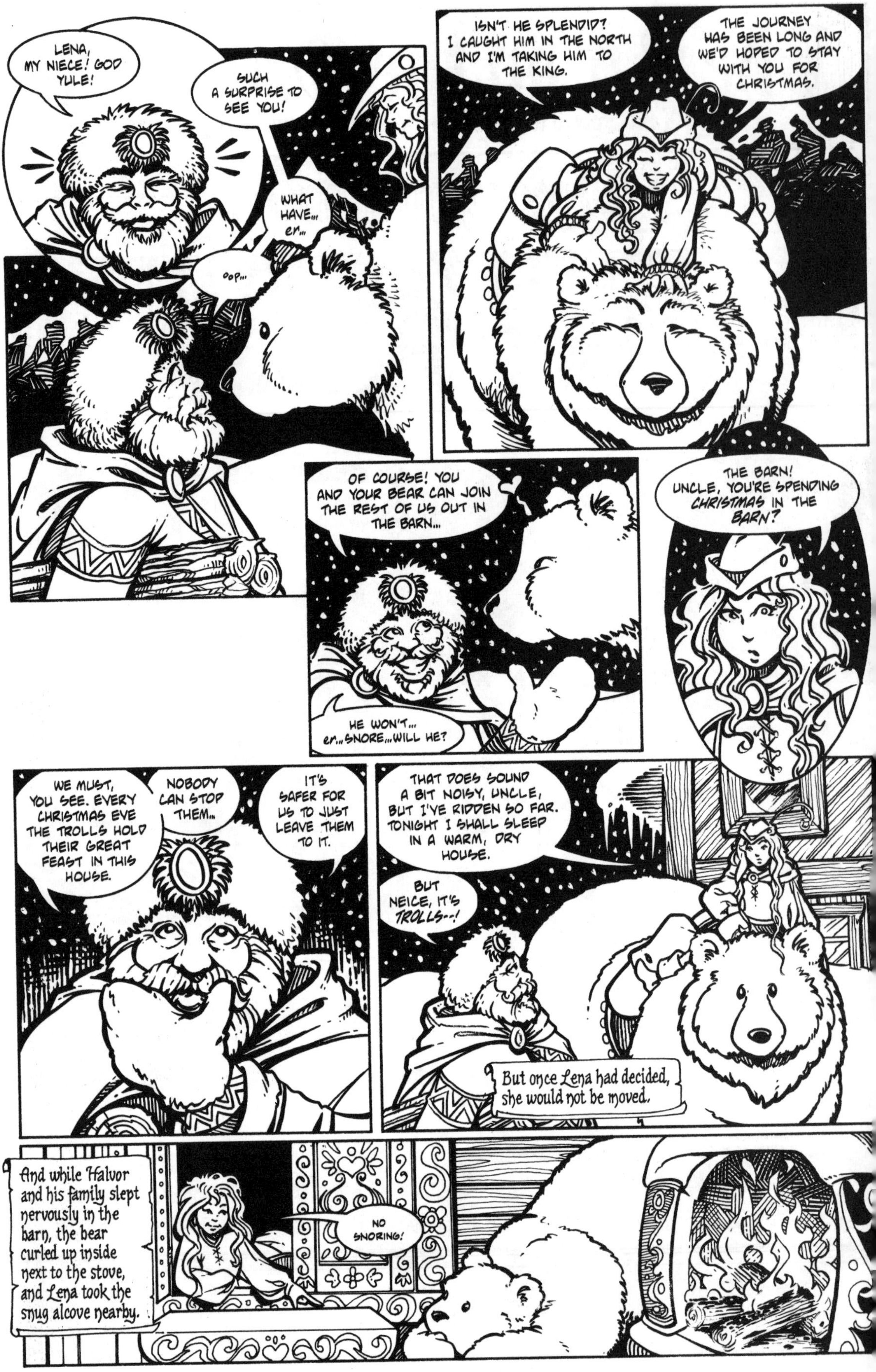

LENA, MY NIECE! GOD YULE!
SUCH A SURPRISE TO SEE YOU!
WHAT HAVE... er...
OOP...
ISN'T HE SPLENDID? I CAUGHT HIM IN THE NORTH AND I'M TAKING HIM TO THE KING.
THE JOURNEY HAS BEEN LONG AND WE'D HOPED TO STAY WITH YOU FOR CHRISTMAS.
OF COURSE! YOU AND YOUR BEAR CAN JOIN THE REST OF US OUT IN THE BARN...
HE WON'T... er... SNORE... WILL HE?
THE BARN! UNCLE, YOU'RE SPENDING CHRISTMAS IN THE BARN?
WE MUST, YOU SEE. EVERY CHRISTMAS EVE THE TROLLS HOLD THEIR GREAT FEAST IN THIS HOUSE.
NOBODY CAN STOP THEM...
IT'S SAFER FOR US TO JUST LEAVE THEM TO IT.
THAT DOES SOUND A BIT NOISY, UNCLE, BUT I'VE RIDDEN SO FAR. TONIGHT I SHALL SLEEP IN A WARM, DRY HOUSE.
BUT NEICE, IT'S TROLLS--!
But once Lena had decided, she would not be moved.
And while Halvor and his family slept nervously in the barn, the bear curled up inside next to the stove, and Lena took the snug alcove nearby.
NO SNORING!

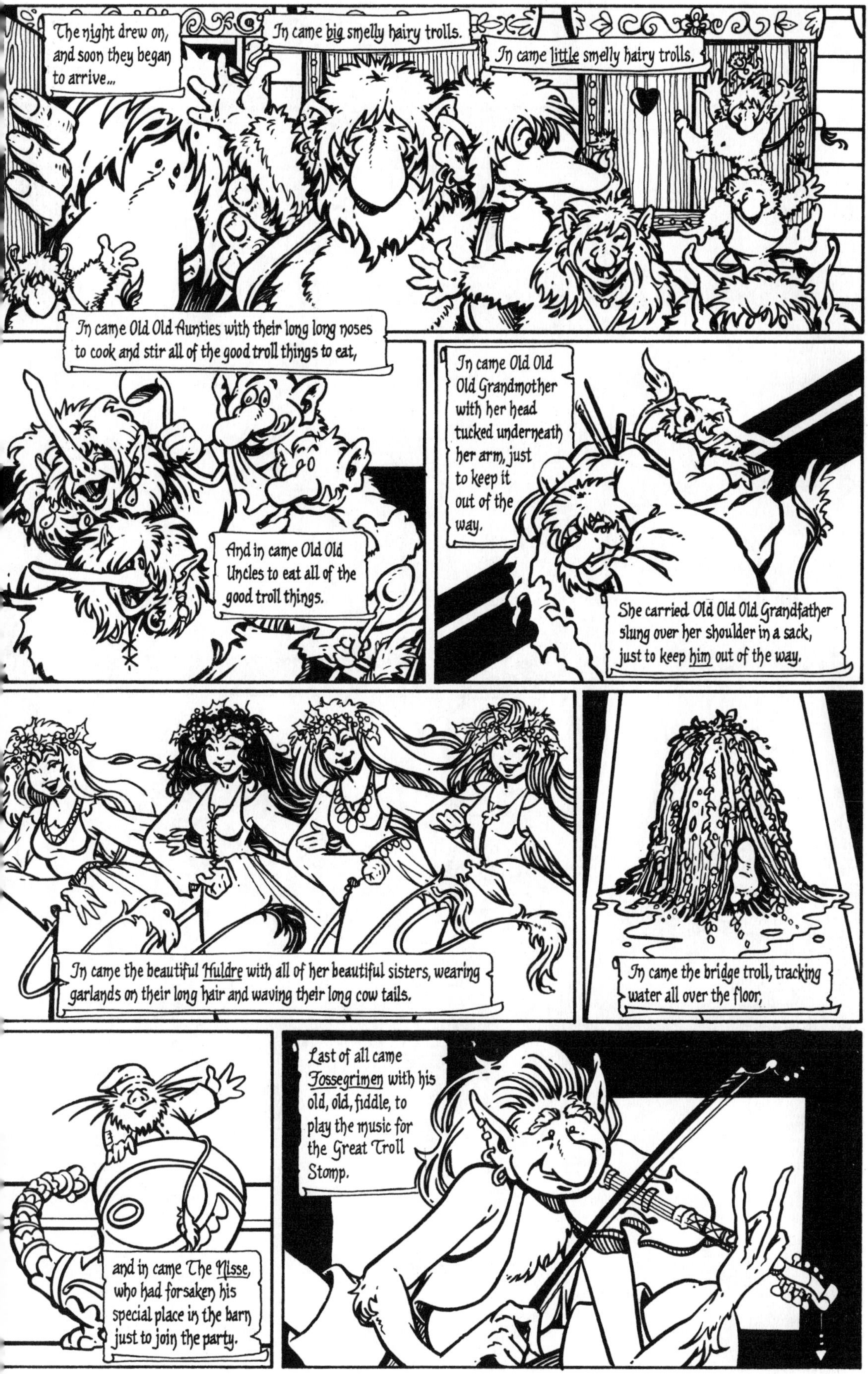
The night drew on, and soon they began to arrive...
In came big smelly hairy trolls.
In came little smelly hairy trolls.
In came Old Old Aunties with their long long noses to cook and stir all of the good troll things to eat,
And in came Old Old Uncles to eat all of the good troll things.
In came Old Old Grandmother with her head tucked underneath her arm, just to keep it out of the way.
She carried Old Old Old Grandfather slung over her shoulder in a sack, just to keep him out of the way.
In came the beautiful Huldre with all of her beautiful sisters, wearing garlands on their long hair and waving their long cow tails.
In came the bridge troll, tracking water all over the floor,
and in came The Nisse, who had forsaken his special place in the barn just to join the party.
Last of all came Fossegrimen with his old, old, fiddle, to play the music for the Great Troll Stomp.

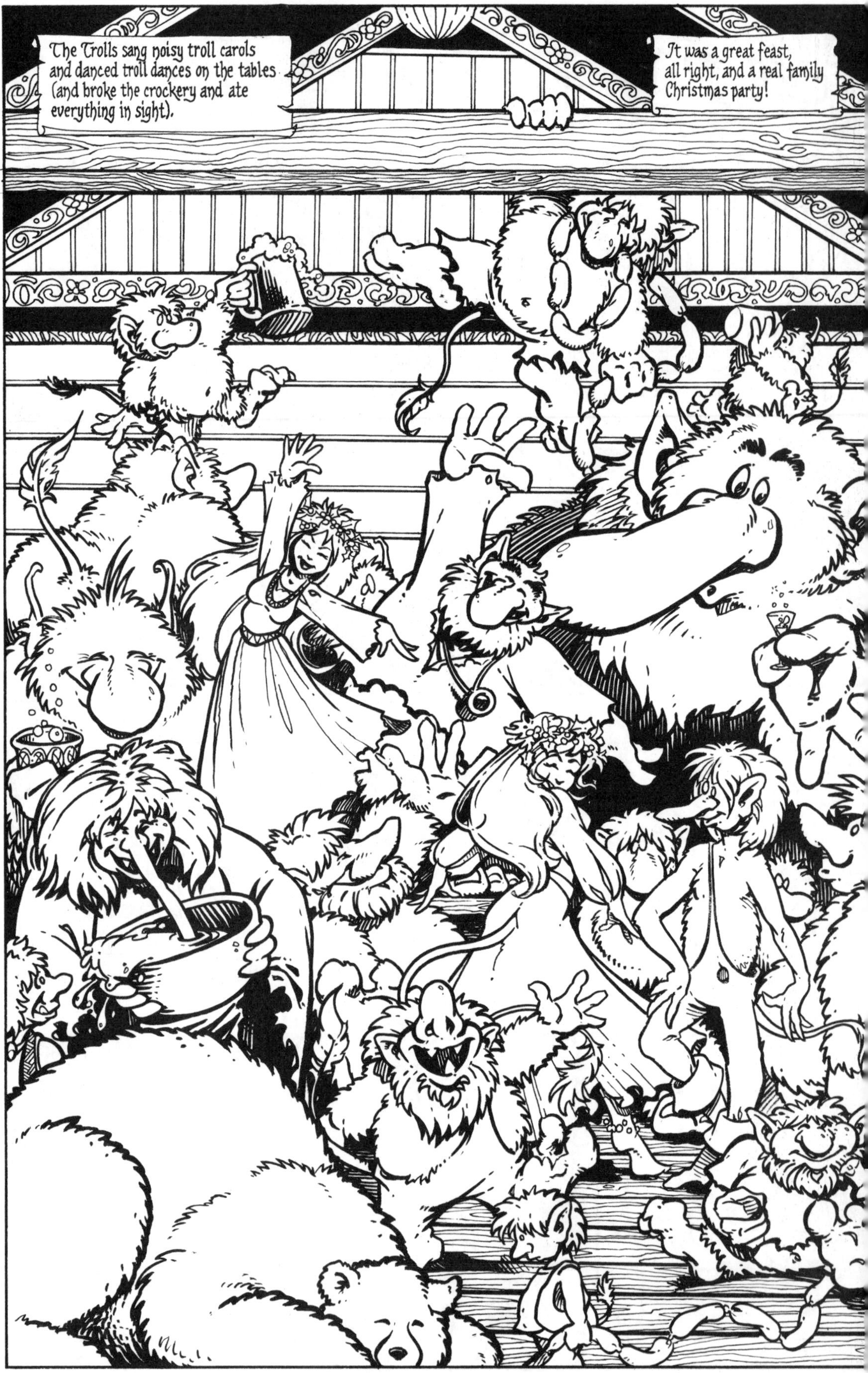
The Trolls sang noisy troll carols and danced troll dances on the tables (and broke the crockery and ate everything in sight).
It was a great feast, all right, and a real family Christmas party!

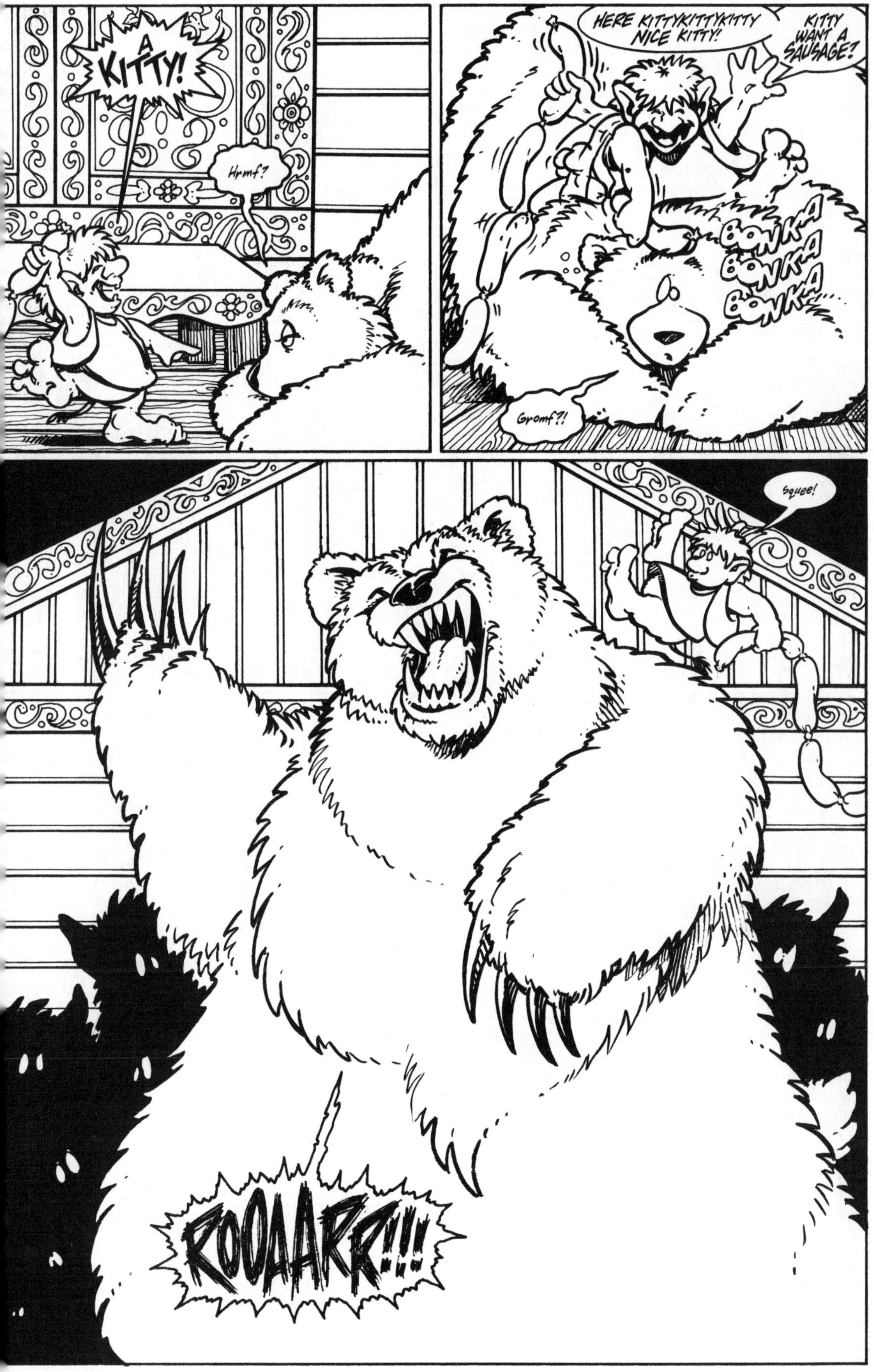
A KITTY!
Hrmf?
HERE KITTYKITTYKITTY NICE KITTY!
KITTY WANT A SAUSAGE?
BONKA BONKA BONKA
Gromf?!
Squee!
ROOAARR!!!

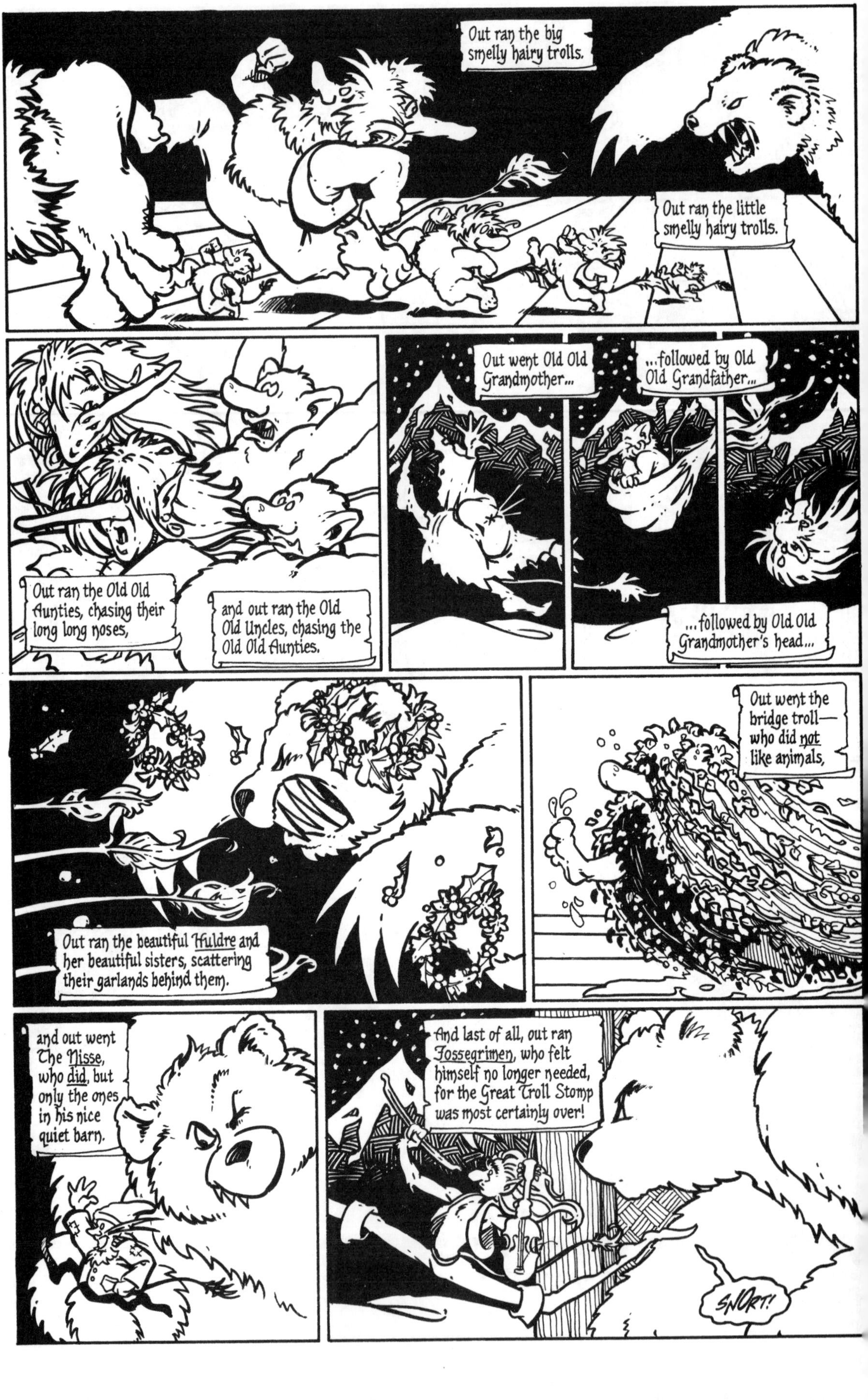

Out ran the big smelly hairy trolls.
Out ran the little smelly hairy trolls.
Out ran the Old Old Aunties, chasing their long long noses,
and out ran the Old Old Uncles, chasing the Old Old Aunties.
Out went Old Old Grandmother...
...followed by Old Old Grandfather...
...followed by Old Old Grandmother's head...
Out ran the beautiful Huldre and her beautiful sisters, scattering their garlands behind them.
Out went the bridge troll— who did not like animals,
and out went The Nisse, who did, but only the ones in his nice quiet barn.
And last of all, out ran Fossegrimen, who felt himself no longer needed, for the Great Troll Stomp was most certainly over!
SNORT!

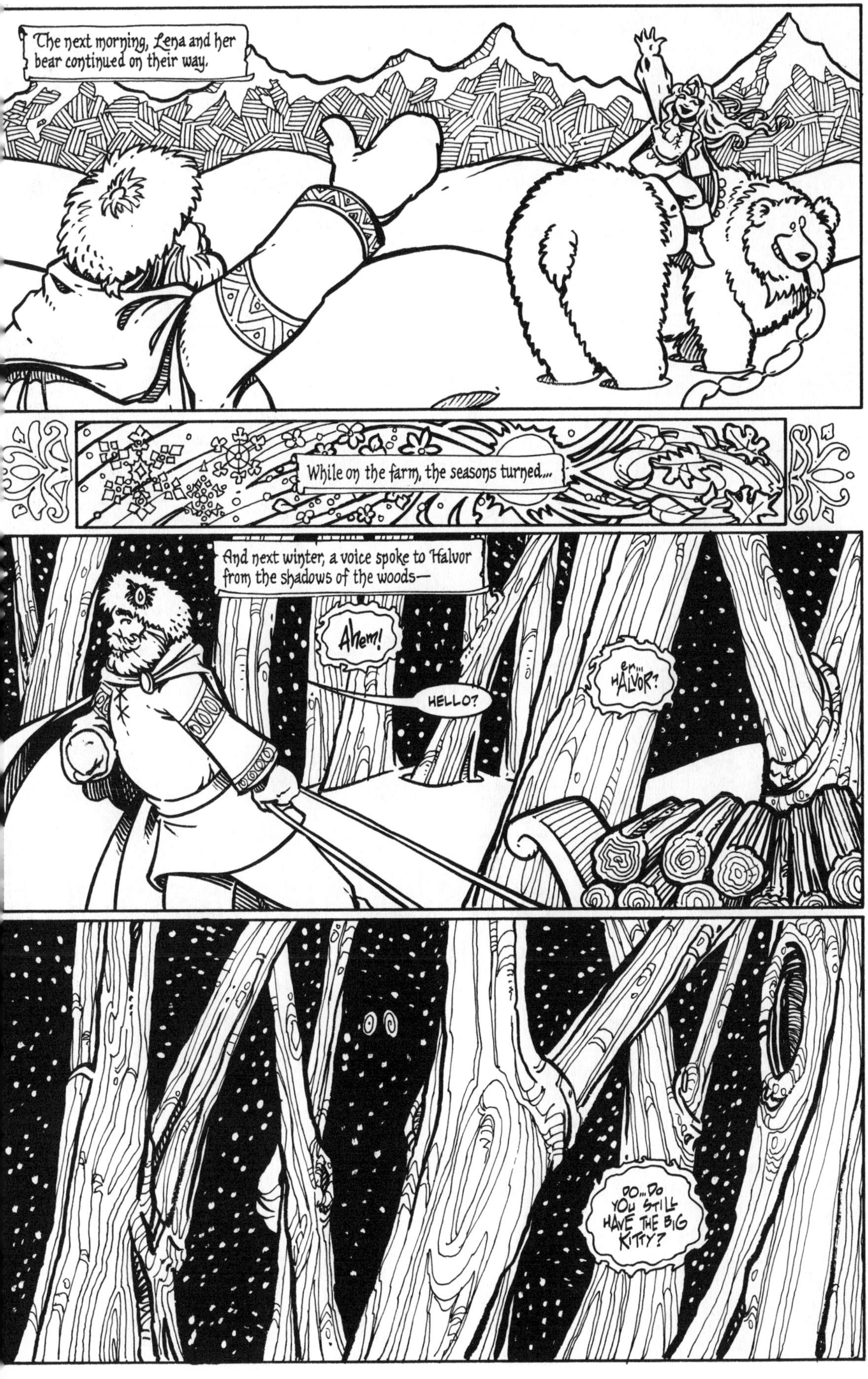
The next morning, Lena and her bear continued on their way.
While on the farm, the seasons turned...
And next winter, a voice spoke to Halvor from the shadows of the woods—
Ahem!
HELLO?
er... HALVOR?
DO... DO YOU STILL HAVE THE BIG KITTY?

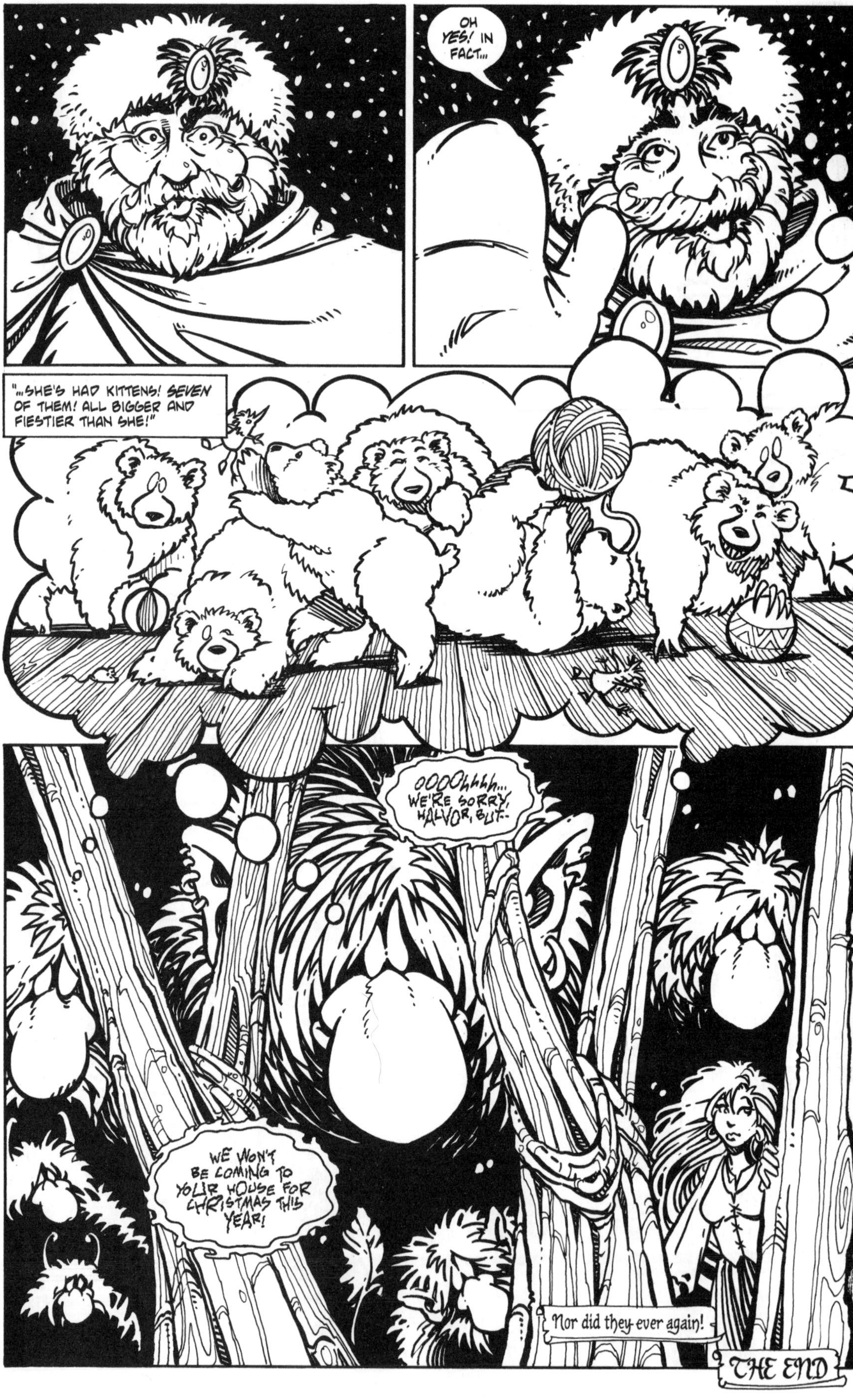
OH YES! IN FACT...
"...SHE'S HAD KITTENS! SEVEN OF THEM! ALL BIGGER AND FIESTIER THAN SHE!"
OOOOhhhh... WE'RE SORRY, HALVOR, BUT-
WE WON'T BE COMING TO YOUR HOUSE FOR CHRISTMAS THIS YEAR!
Nor did they ever again!
THE END

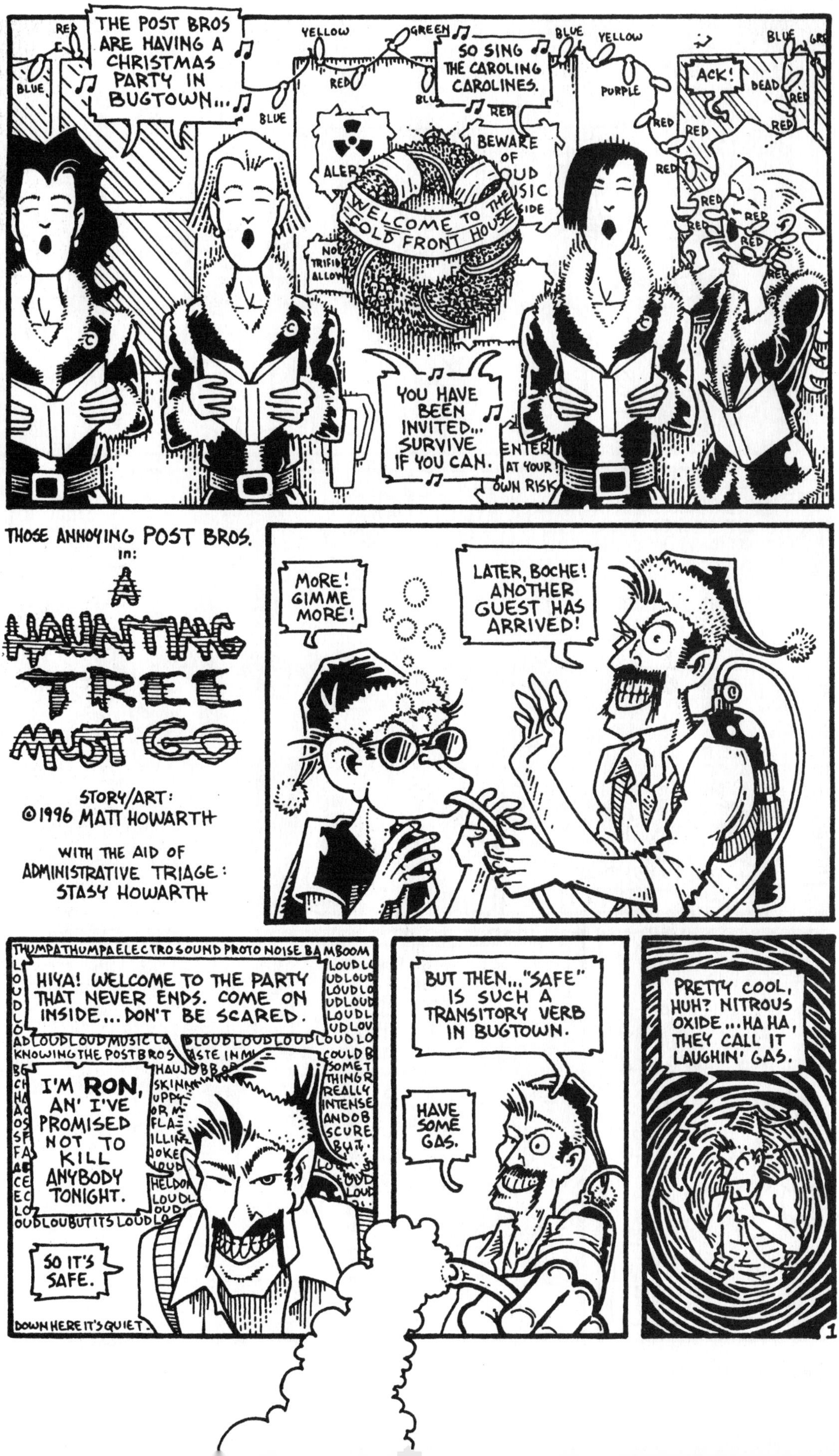

THE POST BROS ARE HAVING A CHRISTMAS PARTY IN BUGTOWN...
SO SING THE CAROLING CAROLINES.
ACK!
WELCOME TO THE COLD FRONT HOUSE
BEWARE OF LOUD MUSIC INSIDE
YOU HAVE BEEN INVITED... SURVIVE IF YOU CAN.
ENTER AT YOUR OWN RISK
THOSE ANNOYING POST BROS. in:
A HAUNTING TREE MUST GO
STORY/ART: ©1996 MATT HOWARTH
WITH THE AID OF ADMINISTRATIVE TRIAGE: STASY HOWARTH
MORE! GIMME MORE!
LATER, BOCHE! ANOTHER GUEST HAS ARRIVED!
THUMPATHUMPAELECTROSOUNDPROTONOISEBAMBOOM
HIYA! WELCOME TO THE PARTY THAT NEVER ENDS. COME ON INSIDE... DON'T BE SCARED.
I'M RON, AN' I'VE PROMISED NOT TO KILL ANYBODY TONIGHT.
SO IT'S SAFE.
DOWN HERE IT'S QUIET.
BUT THEN... "SAFE" IS SUCH A TRANSITORY VERB IN BUGTOWN.
HAVE SOME GAS.
PRETTY COOL, HUH? NITROUS OXIDE... HA HA, THEY CALL IT LAUGHIN' GAS.

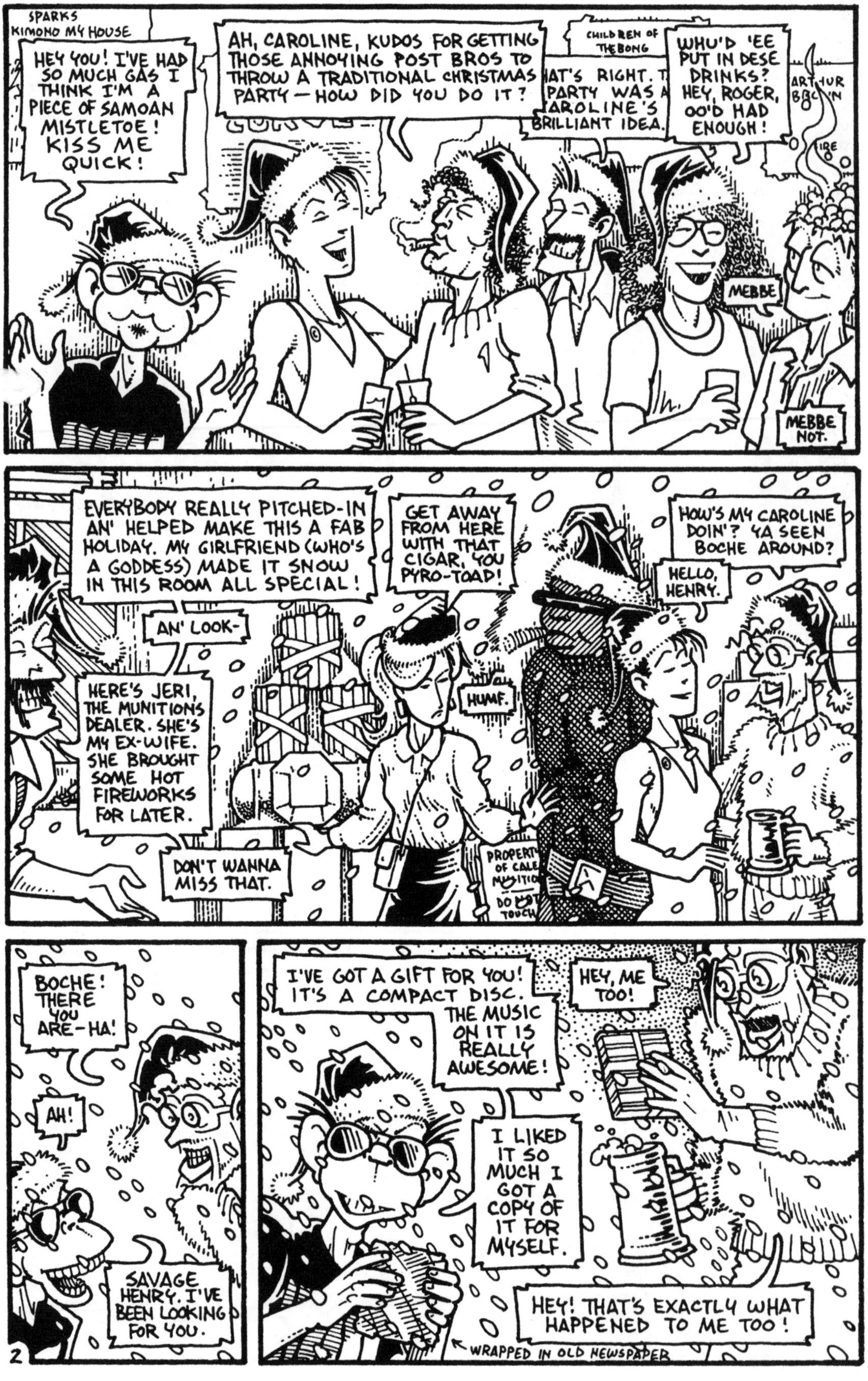
SPARKS
KIMONO MY HOUSE
HEY YOU! I'VE HAD SO MUCH GAS I THINK I'M A PIECE OF SAMOAN MISTLETOE! KISS ME QUICK!
AH, CAROLINE, KUDOS FOR GETTING THOSE ANNOYING POST BROS TO THROW A TRADITIONAL CHRISTMAS PARTY — HOW DID YOU DO IT?
CHILDREN OF THE BONG
HAT'S RIGHT. T PARTY WAS A AROLINE'S BRILLIANT IDEA.
WHU'D 'EE PUT IN DESE DRINKS? HEY, ROGER, OO'D HAD ENOUGH!
MEBBE
MEBBE NOT.
EVERYBODY REALLY PITCHED-IN AN' HELPED MAKE THIS A FAB HOLIDAY. MY GIRLFRIEND (WHO'S A GODDESS) MADE IT SNOW IN THIS ROOM ALL SPECIAL!
AN' LOOK-
HERE'S JERI, THE MUNITIONS DEALER. SHE'S MY EX-WIFE. SHE BROUGHT SOME HOT FIREWORKS FOR LATER.
DON'T WANNA MISS THAT.
GET AWAY FROM HERE WITH THAT CIGAR, YOU PYRO-TOAD!
HUMF.
HELLO, HENRY.
HOW'S MY CAROLINE DOIN'? YA SEEN BOCHE AROUND?
BOCHE! THERE YOU ARE-HA!
AH!
SAVAGE HENRY. I'VE BEEN LOOKING FOR YOU.
I'VE GOT A GIFT FOR YOU! IT'S A COMPACT DISC. THE MUSIC ON IT IS REALLY AWESOME!
I LIKED IT SO MUCH I GOT A COPY OF IT FOR MYSELF.
HEY, ME TOO!
HEY! THAT'S EXACTLY WHAT HAPPENED TO ME TOO!
WRAPPED IN OLD NEWSPAPER

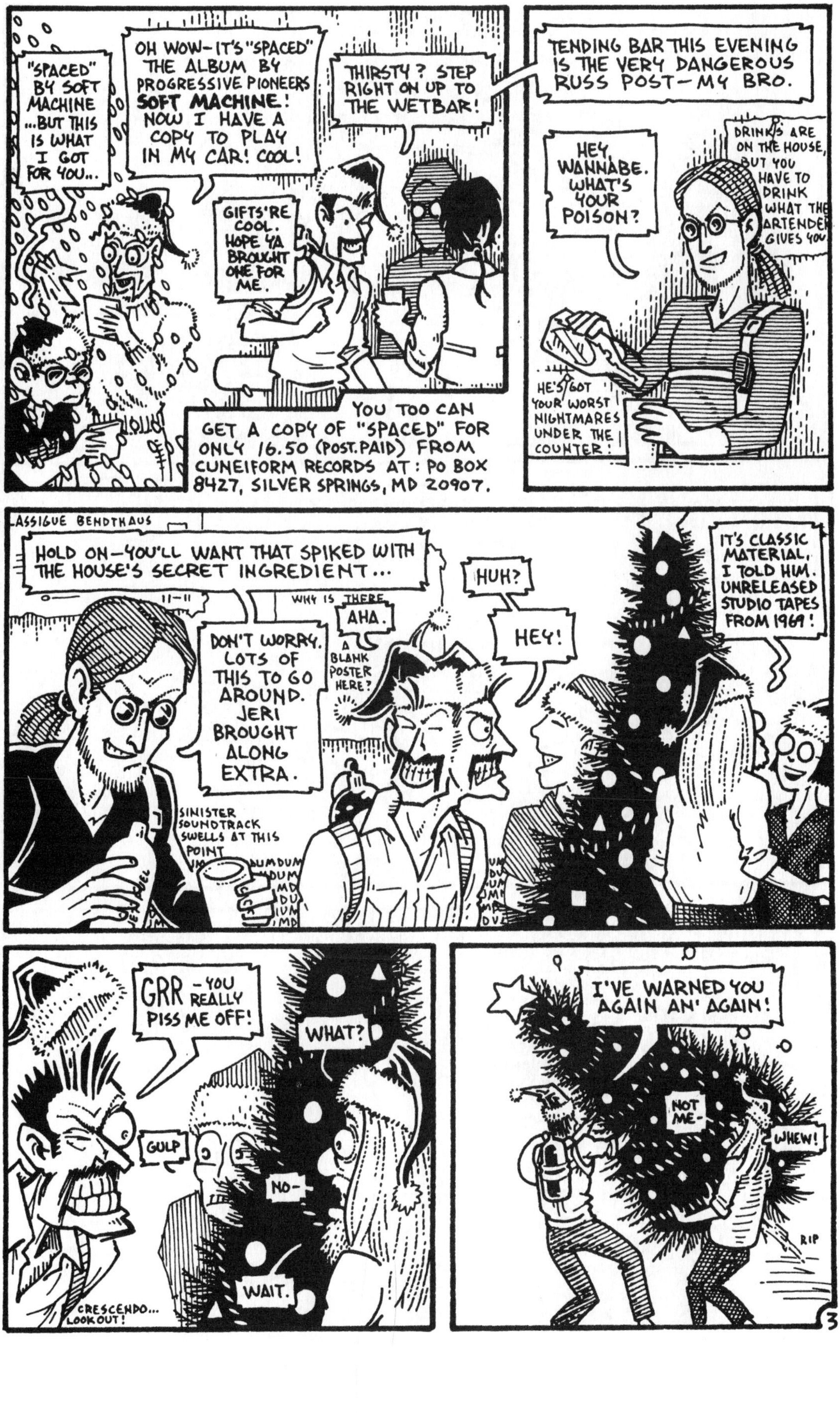
"SPACED" BY SOFT MACHINE ...BUT THIS IS WHAT I GOT FOR YOU...
OH WOW–IT'S "SPACED" THE ALBUM BY PROGRESSIVE PIONEERS SOFT MACHINE! NOW I HAVE A COPY TO PLAY IN MY CAR! COOL!
THIRSTY? STEP RIGHT ON UP TO THE WETBAR!
GIFTS'RE COOL. HOPE YA BROUGHT ONE FOR ME.
YOU TOO CAN GET A COPY OF "SPACED" FOR ONLY 16.50 (POST.PAID) FROM CUNEIFORM RECORDS AT: PO BOX 8427, SILVER SPRINGS, MD 20907.
TENDING BAR THIS EVENING IS THE VERY DANGEROUS RUSS POST–MY BRO.
HEY, WANNABE. WHAT'S YOUR POISON?
DRINKS ARE ON THE HOUSE, BUT YOU HAVE TO DRINK WHAT THE BARTENDER GIVES YOU
HE'S GOT YOUR WORST NIGHTMARES UNDER THE COUNTER!
HOLD ON–YOU'LL WANT THAT SPIKED WITH THE HOUSE'S SECRET INGREDIENT...
DON'T WORRY. LOTS OF THIS TO GO AROUND. JERI BROUGHT ALONG EXTRA.
WHY IS THERE
AHA.
A BLANK POSTER HERE?
HUH?
HEY!
IT'S CLASSIC MATERIAL, I TOLD HIM. UNRELEASED STUDIO TAPES FROM 1969!
SINISTER SOUNDTRACK SWELLS AT THIS POINT
DUMDUM DUM
GRR–YOU REALLY PISS ME OFF!
WHAT?
GULP
NO–
WAIT.
CRESCENDO... LOOKOUT!
I'VE WARNED YOU AGAIN AN' AGAIN!
NOT ME–
WHEW!
RIP

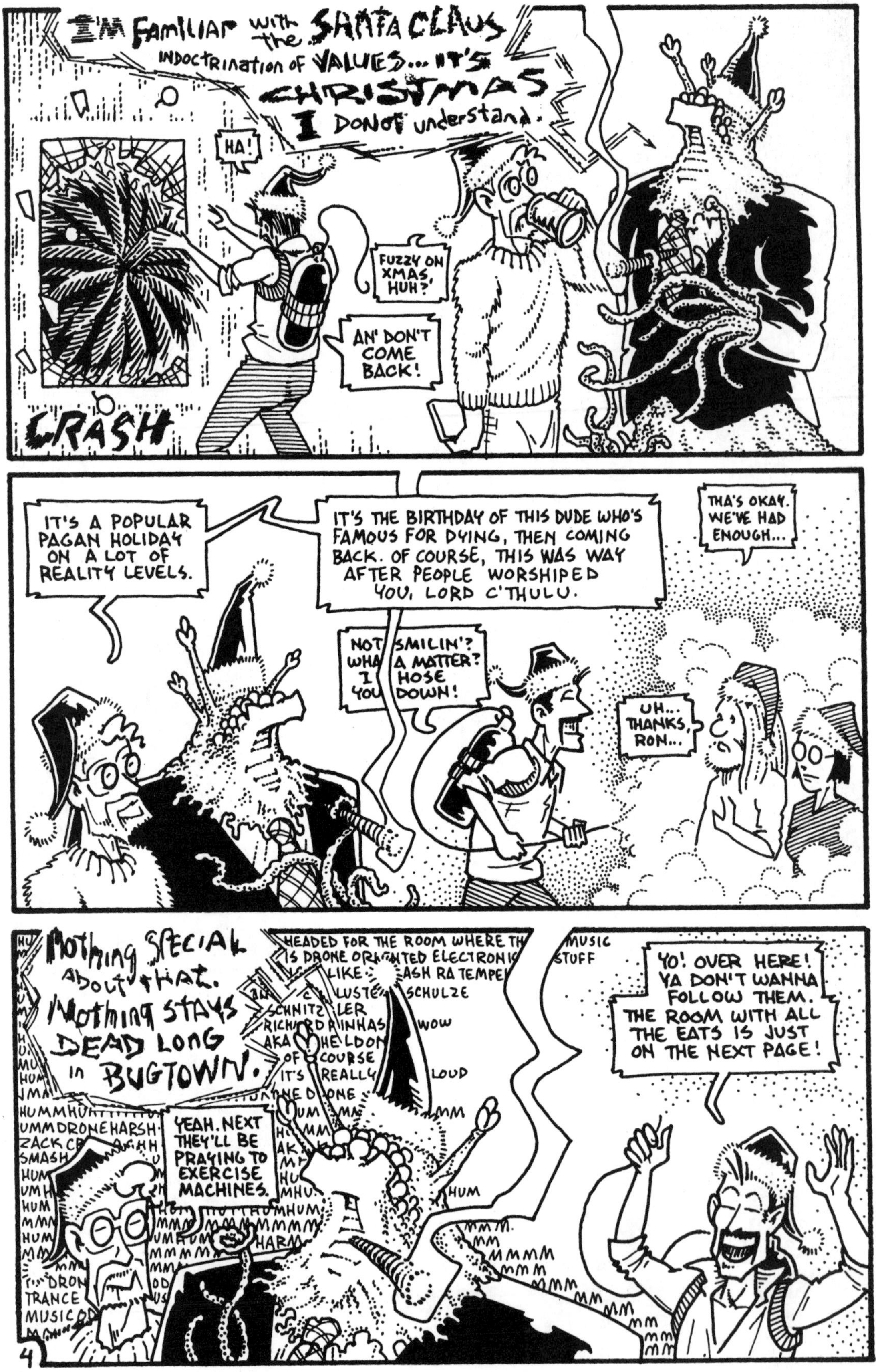
I'M FAMILIAR WITH THE SANTA CLAUS INDOCTRINATION OF VALUES... IT'S CHRISTMAS I DONOT UNDERSTAND.
HA!
FUZZY ON XMAS, HUH?
AN' DON'T COME BACK!
CRASH
IT'S A POPULAR PAGAN HOLIDAY ON A LOT OF REALITY LEVELS.
IT'S THE BIRTHDAY OF THIS DUDE WHO'S FAMOUS FOR DYING, THEN COMING BACK. OF COURSE, THIS WAS WAY AFTER PEOPLE WORSHIPED YOU, LORD C'THULU.
THA'S OKAY. WE'VE HAD ENOUGH...
NOT SMILIN'? WHA A MATTER? I HOSE YOU DOWN!
UH... THANKS, RON...
NOTHING SPECIAL ABOUT THAT. NOTHING STAYS DEAD LONG IN BUGTOWN.
HEADED FOR THE ROOM WHERE TH
IS DRONE OR TED ELECTRONI
LIKE ASH RA TEMPE
LUSTE SCHULZE
SCHNITZ LER
RICH RD INHAS WOW
AKA HE LDON
OF COURSE
IT'S REALLY LOUD
MUSIC
STUFF
YO! OVER HERE! YA DON'T WANNA FOLLOW THEM. THE ROOM WITH ALL THE EATS IS JUST ON THE NEXT PAGE!
HUMMHU
UMMDRONEHARSH
ZACK CR
SMASH
YEAH. NEXT THEY'LL BE PRAYING TO EXERCISE MACHINES.
MMMM
DRON
TRANCE
MUSIC

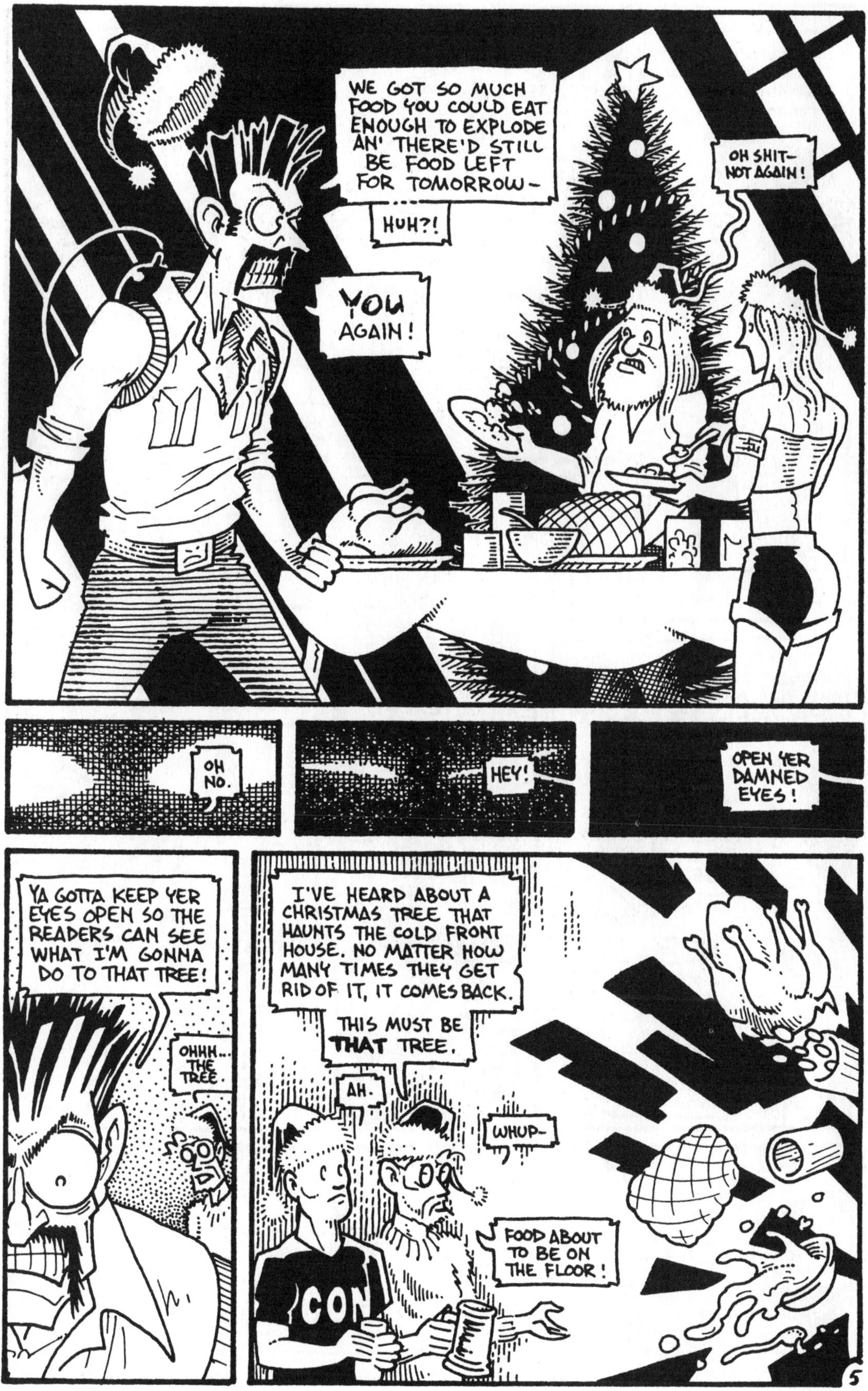
WE GOT SO MUCH FOOD YOU COULD EAT ENOUGH TO EXPLODE AN' THERE'D STILL BE FOOD LEFT FOR TOMORROW-
....
HUH?!
OH SHIT- NOT AGAIN!
YOU AGAIN!
OH NO.
HEY!
OPEN YER DAMNED EYES!
YA GOTTA KEEP YER EYES OPEN SO THE READERS CAN SEE WHAT I'M GONNA DO TO THAT TREE!
OHHH... THE TREE.
I'VE HEARD ABOUT A CHRISTMAS TREE THAT HAUNTS THE COLD FRONT HOUSE. NO MATTER HOW MANY TIMES THEY GET RID OF IT, IT COMES BACK.
THIS MUST BE THAT TREE.
AH.
WHUP-
FOOD ABOUT TO BE ON THE FLOOR!
CON
5

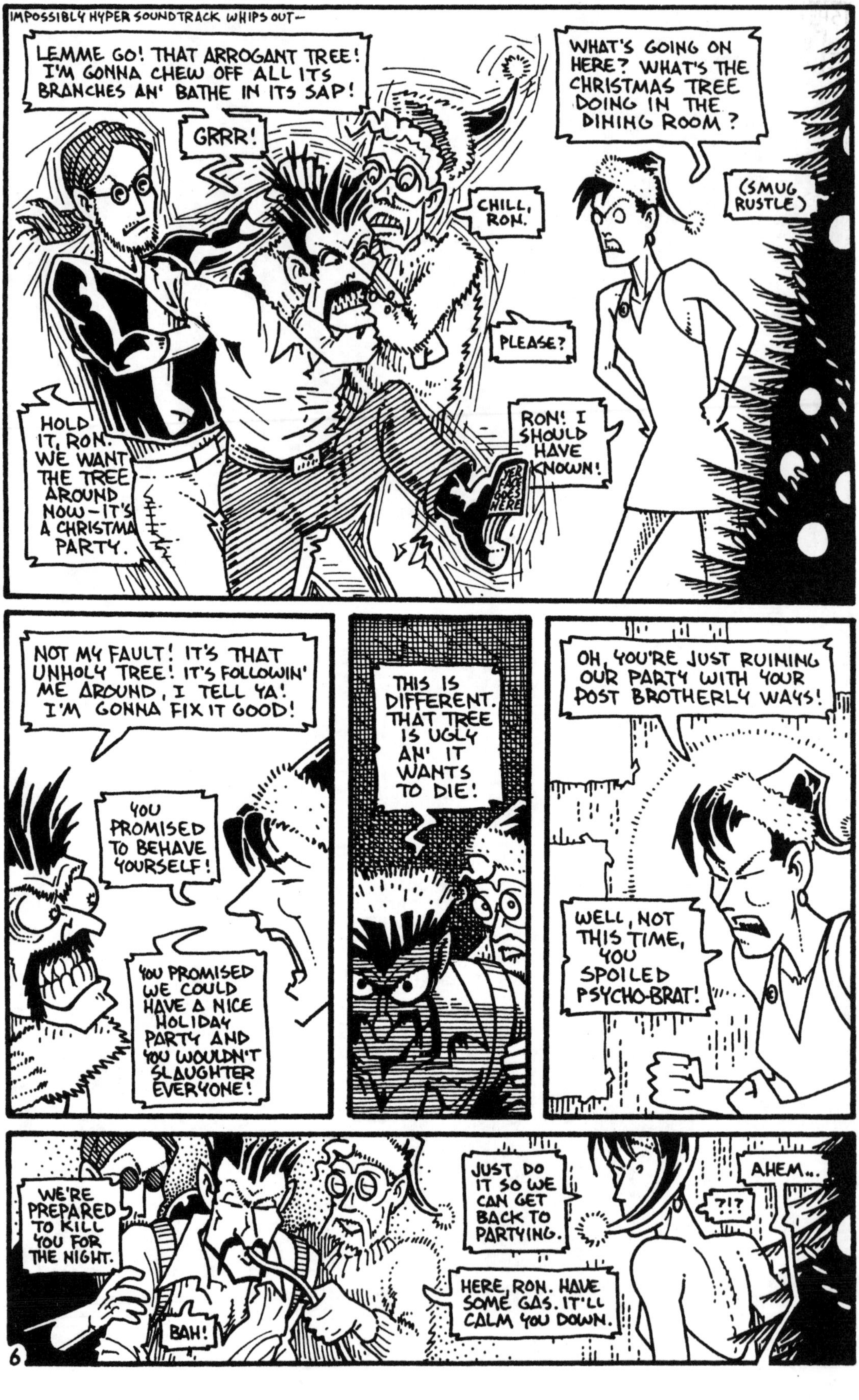
IMPOSSIBLY HYPER SOUNDTRACK WHIPS OUT—
LEMME GO! THAT ARROGANT TREE! I'M GONNA CHEW OFF ALL ITS BRANCHES AN' BATHE IN ITS SAP!
GRRR!
WHAT'S GOING ON HERE? WHAT'S THE CHRISTMAS TREE DOING IN THE DINING ROOM?
(SMUG RUSTLE)
CHILL, RON.
PLEASE?
HOLD IT, RON. WE WANT THE TREE AROUND NOW—IT'S A CHRISTMAS PARTY.
RON! I SHOULD HAVE KNOWN!
NOT MY FAULT! IT'S THAT UNHOLY TREE! IT'S FOLLOWIN' ME AROUND, I TELL YA! I'M GONNA FIX IT GOOD!
YOU PROMISED TO BEHAVE YOURSELF!
YOU PROMISED WE COULD HAVE A NICE HOLIDAY PARTY AND YOU WOULDN'T SLAUGHTER EVERYONE!
THIS IS DIFFERENT. THAT TREE IS UGLY AN' IT WANTS TO DIE!
OH, YOU'RE JUST RUINING OUR PARTY WITH YOUR POST BROTHERLY WAYS!
WELL, NOT THIS TIME, YOU SPOILED PSYCHO-BRAT!
WE'RE PREPARED TO KILL YOU FOR THE NIGHT.
JUST DO IT SO WE CAN GET BACK TO PARTYING.
AHEM...
?!?
HERE, RON. HAVE SOME GAS. IT'LL CALM YOU DOWN.
BAH!

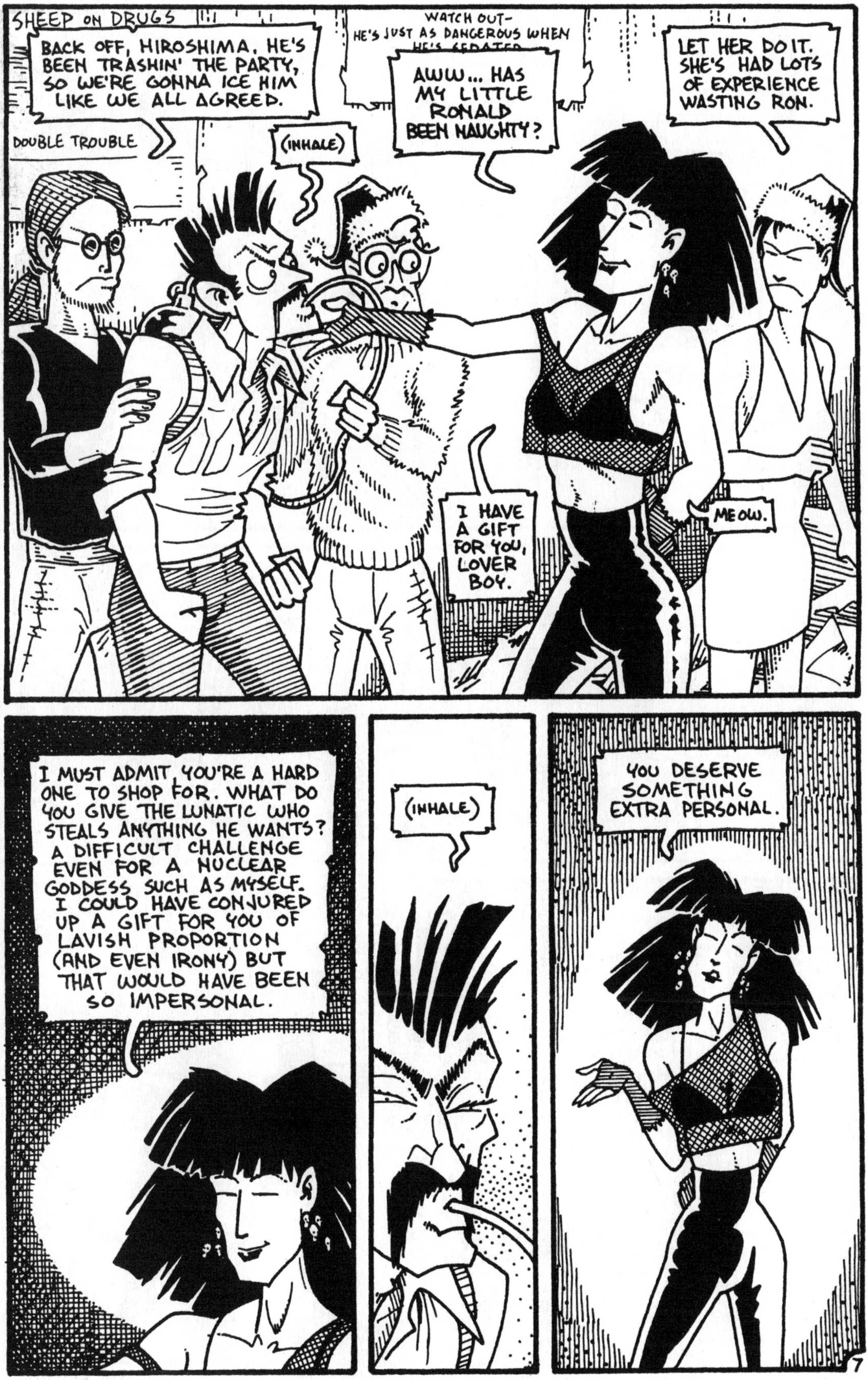
SHEEP ON DRUGS
BACK OFF, HIROSHIMA. HE'S BEEN TRASHIN' THE PARTY, SO WE'RE GONNA ICE HIM LIKE WE ALL AGREED.
DOUBLE TROUBLE
(INHALE)
WATCH OUT-
HE'S JUST AS DANGEROUS WHEN
AWW... HAS MY LITTLE RONALD BEEN NAUGHTY?
LET HER DO IT. SHE'S HAD LOTS OF EXPERIENCE WASTING RON.
I HAVE A GIFT FOR YOU, LOVER BOY.
MEOW.
I MUST ADMIT, YOU'RE A HARD ONE TO SHOP FOR. WHAT DO YOU GIVE THE LUNATIC WHO STEALS ANYTHING HE WANTS? A DIFFICULT CHALLENGE EVEN FOR A NUCLEAR GODDESS SUCH AS MYSELF. I COULD HAVE CONJURED UP A GIFT FOR YOU OF LAVISH PROPORTION (AND EVEN IRONY) BUT THAT WOULD HAVE BEEN SO IMPERSONAL.
(INHALE)
YOU DESERVE SOMETHING EXTRA PERSONAL.

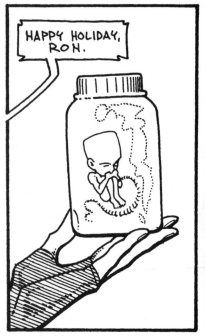

HAPPY HOLIDAY, RON.

OH - **COOL**! LOOKIT ITS TINY LITTLE PUCKERFACE!

LEMME SEE.

I MADE IT FOR YOU MYSELF.

I'M SURPRISED AT YOU, RUSS. YOU GREW UP WITH HIM—YOU KNOW NOT TO PROVOKE HIM. YOU HAVE TO DISTRACT HIM WITH A NEW TOY.

HA HA HA!

HE DOESN'T STAY DISTRACTED FOR LONG.

THEN KEEP HIM AMUSED OR WE'LL HAVE TO KILL HIM.

AWW...HEY, YOU GUYS...

COME ALONG NOW. YOU'RE NOT WASTED ENOUGH FOR THIS. LET ME GET YOU ANOTHER OF THOSE SPECIAL HOUSE DRINKS.

RON SPILLED MY DRINK ON THE CHRISTMAS TREE. THEN HE TORCHED IT, AND NOW HE'S TOASTING YOUR GIFT ON A STICK ...AND... HE WON'T SHARE ANY WITH ME...

PRETTY SMALL TO SHARE.

AWW... TOO LATE.

AN INDOOR FIRE? I'LL KILL HIM WITH MY BARE TEETH!

IT'S THE END FOR YOU.

8

IT ENDS HERE BECAUSE JERI'S FIREWORKS GO OFF, BLOWING THE HOUSE TO BITS. IT WILL TAKE EVERYONE UNTIL LONG AFTER NEW YEARS TO REGENERATE.

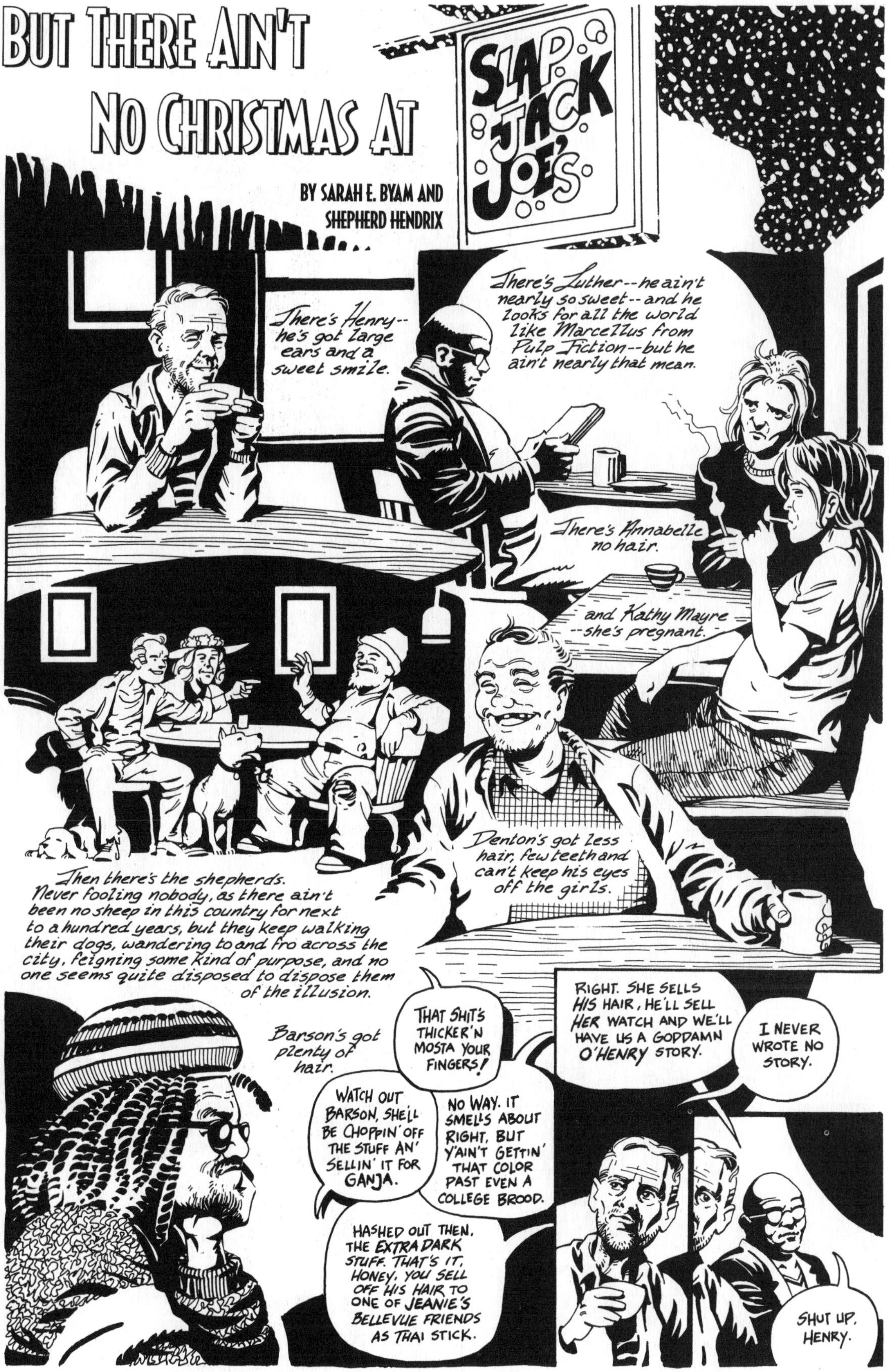

BUT THERE AIN'T NO CHRISTMAS AT
SLAP JACK JOE'S
BY SARAH E. BYAM AND SHEPHERD HENDRIX
There's Henry-- he's got large ears and a sweet smile.
There's Luther--he ain't nearly so sweet--and he looks for all the world like Marcellus from Pulp Fiction--but he ain't nearly that mean.
There's Annabelle no hair.
and Kathy Mayre --she's pregnant.
Denton's got less hair, few teeth and can't keep his eyes off the girls.
Then there's the shepherds. Never fooling nobody, as there ain't been no sheep in this country for next to a hundred years, but they keep walking their dogs, wandering to and fro across the city, feigning some kind of purpose, and no one seems quite disposed to dispose them of the illusion.
Barson's got plenty of hair.
THAT SHIT'S THICKER'N MOSTA YOUR FINGERS!
WATCH OUT BARSON, SHE'LL BE CHOPPIN' OFF THE STUFF AN' SELLIN' IT FOR GANJA.
NO WAY. IT SMELLS ABOUT RIGHT, BUT Y'AIN'T GETTIN' THAT COLOR PAST EVEN A COLLEGE BROOD.
HASHED OUT THEN. THE EXTRA DARK STUFF. THAT'S IT, HONEY, YOU SELL OFF HIS HAIR TO ONE OF JEANIE'S BELLEVUE FRIENDS AS THAI STICK.
RIGHT. SHE SELLS HIS HAIR, HE'LL SELL HER WATCH AND WE'LL HAVE US A GODDAMN O'HENRY STORY.
I NEVER WROTE NO STORY.
SHUT UP, HENRY.

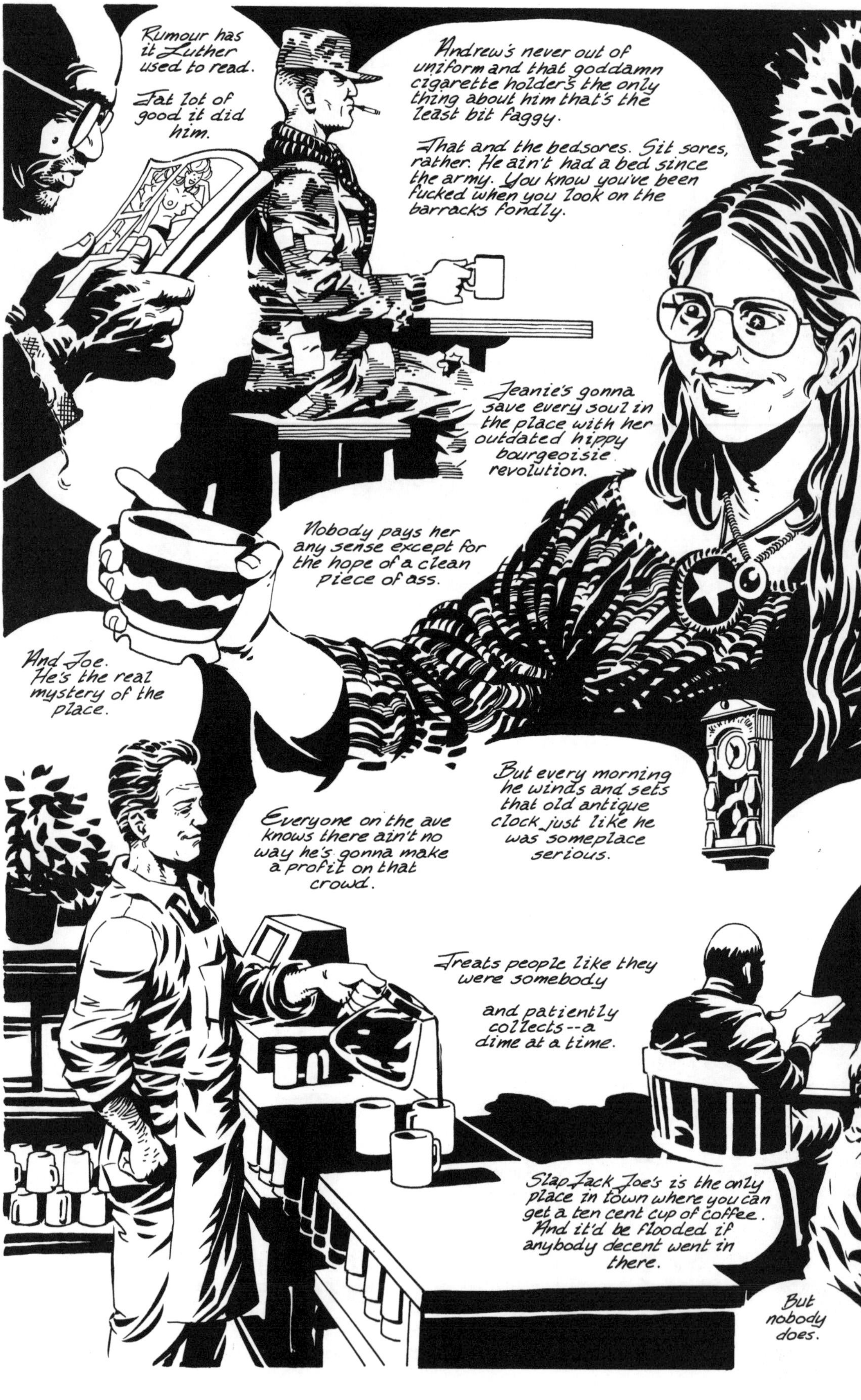
Rumour has it Luther used to read.
Fat lot of good it did him.
Andrew's never out of uniform and that goddamn cigarette holder's the only thing about him that's the least bit faggy.
That and the bedsores. Sit sores, rather. He ain't had a bed since the army. You know you've been fucked when you look on the barracks fondly.
Jeanie's gonna save every soul in the place with her outdated hippy bourgeoisie revolution.
Nobody pays her any sense except for the hope of a clean piece of ass.
And Joe. He's the real mystery of the place.
Everyone on the ave knows there ain't no way he's gonna make a profit on that crowd.
But every morning he winds and sets that old antique clock just like he was someplace serious.
Treats people like they were somebody
and patiently collects--a dime at a time.
SlapJack Joe's is the only place in town where you can get a ten cent cup of coffee. And it'd be flooded if anybody decent went in there.
But nobody does.

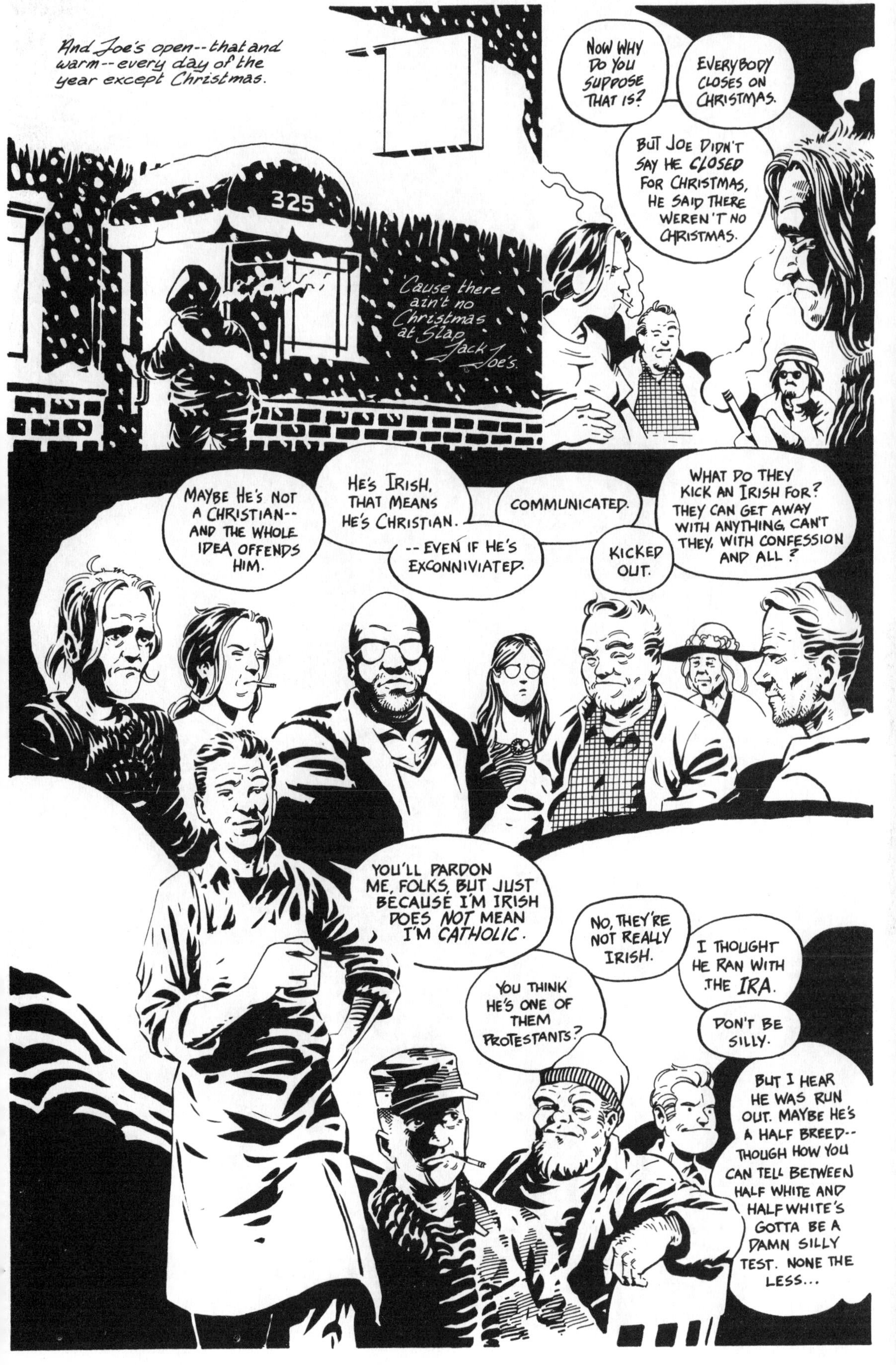
And Joe's open--that and warm--every day of the year except Christmas.
'Cause there ain't no Christmas at Slap Jack Joe's.
Now why do you suppose that is?
Everybody closes on Christmas.
But Joe didn't say he closed for Christmas, he said there weren't no Christmas.
Maybe he's not a Christian--and the whole idea offends him.
He's Irish, that means he's Christian.
--even if he's exconniviated.
Communicated.
Kicked out.
What do they kick an Irish for? They can get away with anything, can't they, with confession and all?
You'll pardon me, folks, but just because I'm Irish does not mean I'm Catholic.
No, they're not really Irish.
I thought he ran with the IRA.
You think he's one of them Protestants?
Don't be silly.
But I hear he was run out. Maybe he's a half breed--though how you can tell between half white and half white's gotta be a damn silly test. None the less...

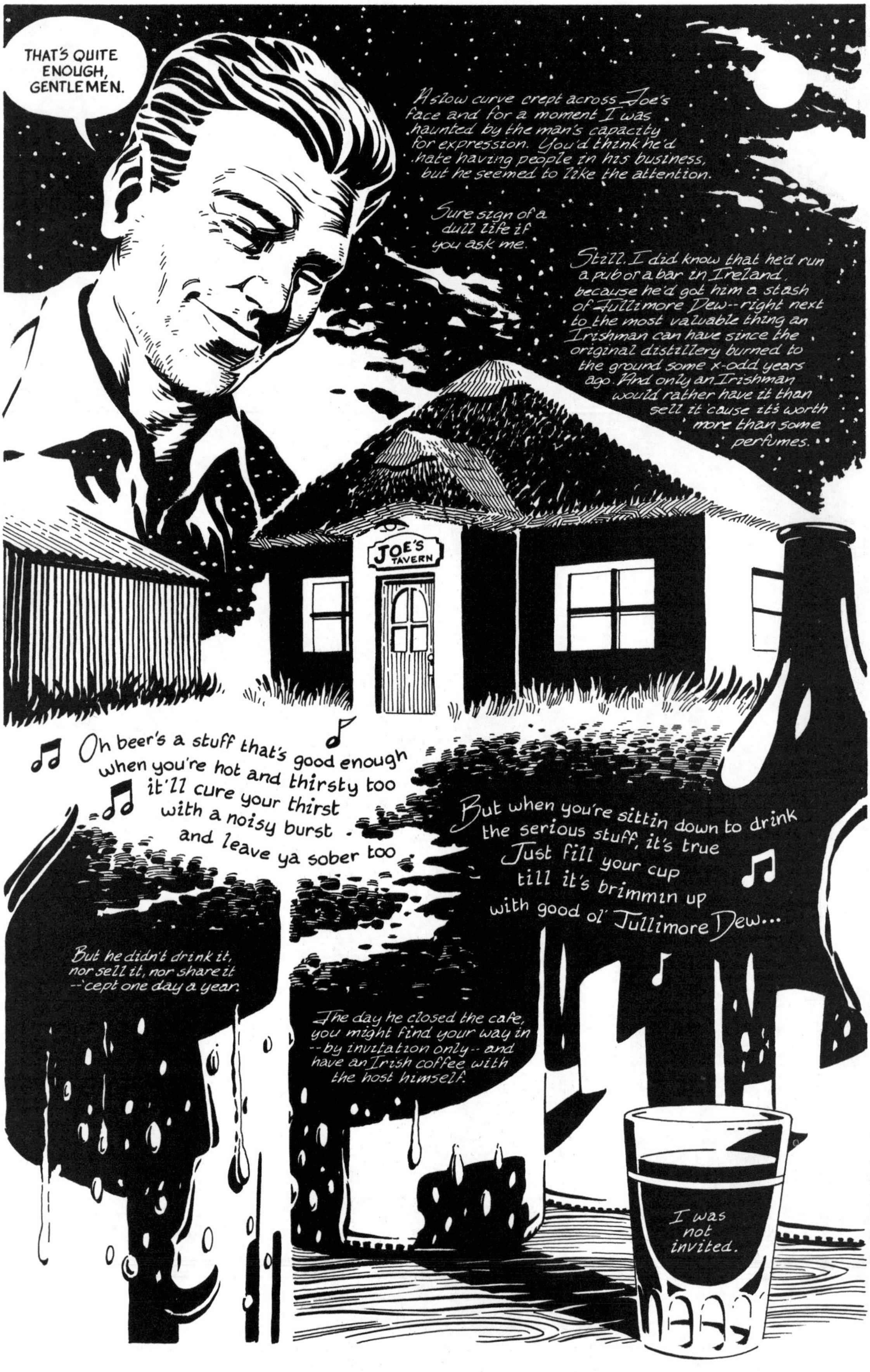

THAT'S QUITE ENOUGH, GENTLEMEN.
A slow curve crept across Joe's face and for a moment I was haunted by the man's capacity for expression. You'd think he'd hate having people in his business, but he seemed to like the attention.
Sure sign of a dull life if you ask me.
Still. I did know that he'd run a pub or a bar in Ireland, because he'd got him a stash of Tullimore Dew--right next to the most valuable thing an Irishman can have since the original distillery burned to the ground some x-odd years ago. And only an Irishman would rather have it than sell it 'cause it's worth more than some perfumes.
JOE'S TAVERN
Oh beer's a stuff that's good enough when you're hot and thirsty too it'll cure your thirst with a noisy burst and leave ya sober too
But when you're sittin down to drink the serious stuff, it's true Just fill your cup till it's brimmin up with good ol' Tullimore Dew...
But he didn't drink it, nor sell it, nor share it --'cept one day a year.
The day he closed the cafe, you might find your way in --by invitation only-- and have an Irish coffee with the host himself.
I was not invited.

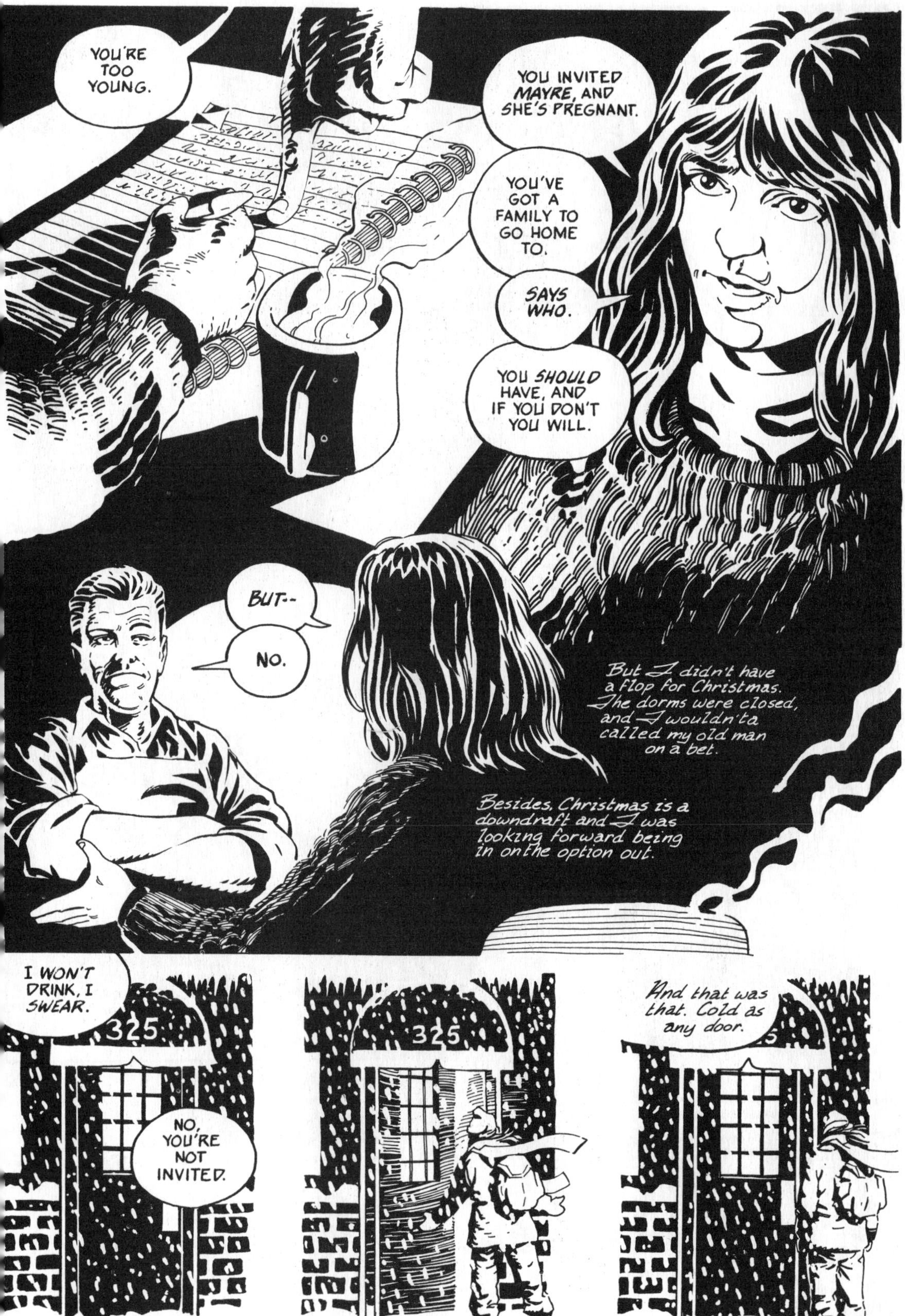
YOU'RE TOO YOUNG.
YOU INVITED MAYRE, AND SHE'S PREGNANT.
YOU'VE GOT A FAMILY TO GO HOME TO.
SAYS WHO.
YOU SHOULD HAVE, AND IF YOU DON'T YOU WILL.
BUT--
NO.
But I didn't have a flop for Christmas. The dorms were closed, and I wouldn'ta called my old man on a bet.
Besides, Christmas is a downdraft and I was looking forward being in on the option out.
I WON'T DRINK, I SWEAR.
325
NO, YOU'RE NOT INVITED.
325
And that was that. Cold as any door.

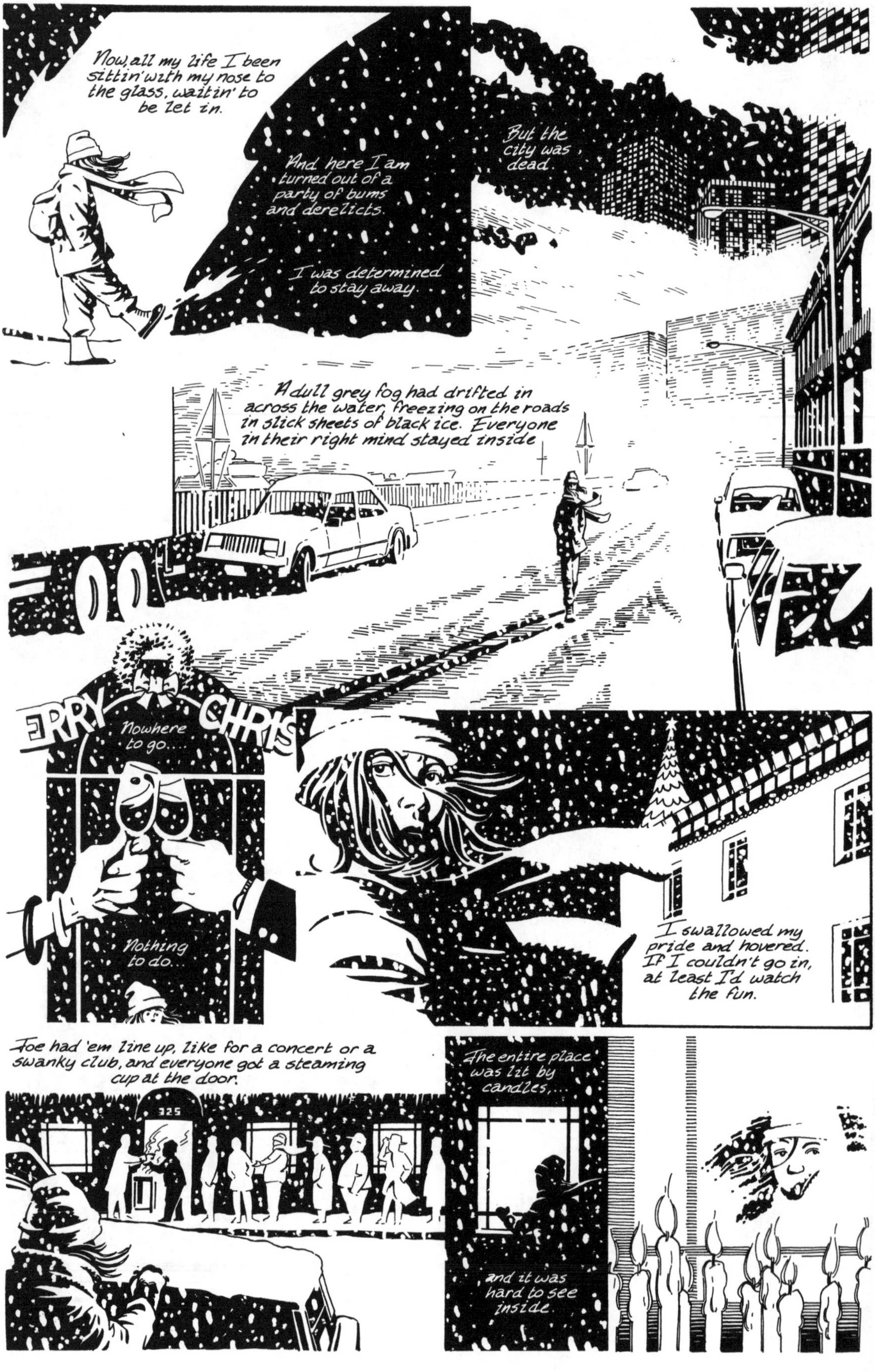
Now, all my life I been sittin' with my nose to the glass, waitin' to be let in.
And here I am turned out of a party of bums and derelicts.
I was determined to stay away.
But the city was dead.
A dull grey fog had drifted in across the water, freezing on the roads in slick sheets of black ice. Everyone in their right mind stayed inside
ERRY CHRIS
Nowhere to go....
Nothing to do...
I swallowed my pride and hovered. If I couldn't go in, at least I'd watch the fun.
Joe had 'em line up, like for a concert or a swanky club, and everyone got a steaming cup at the door.
325
The entire place was lit by candles,...
and it was hard to see inside.

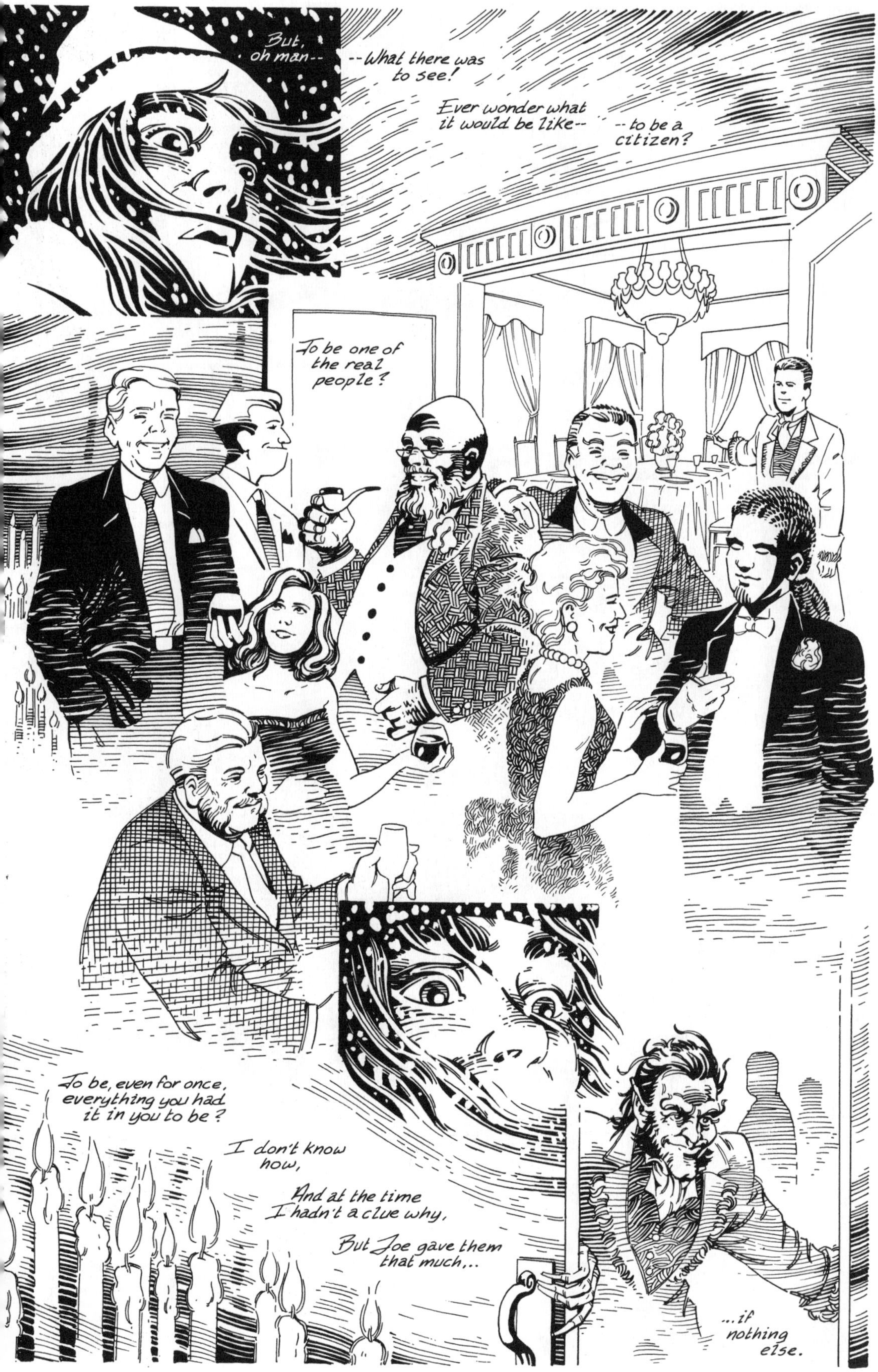

But, oh man--
--What there was to see!
Ever wonder what it would be like--
--to be a citizen?
To be one of the real people?
To be, even for once, everything you had it in you to be?
I don't know how,
And at the time I hadn't a clue why,
But Joe gave them that much...
...if nothing else.

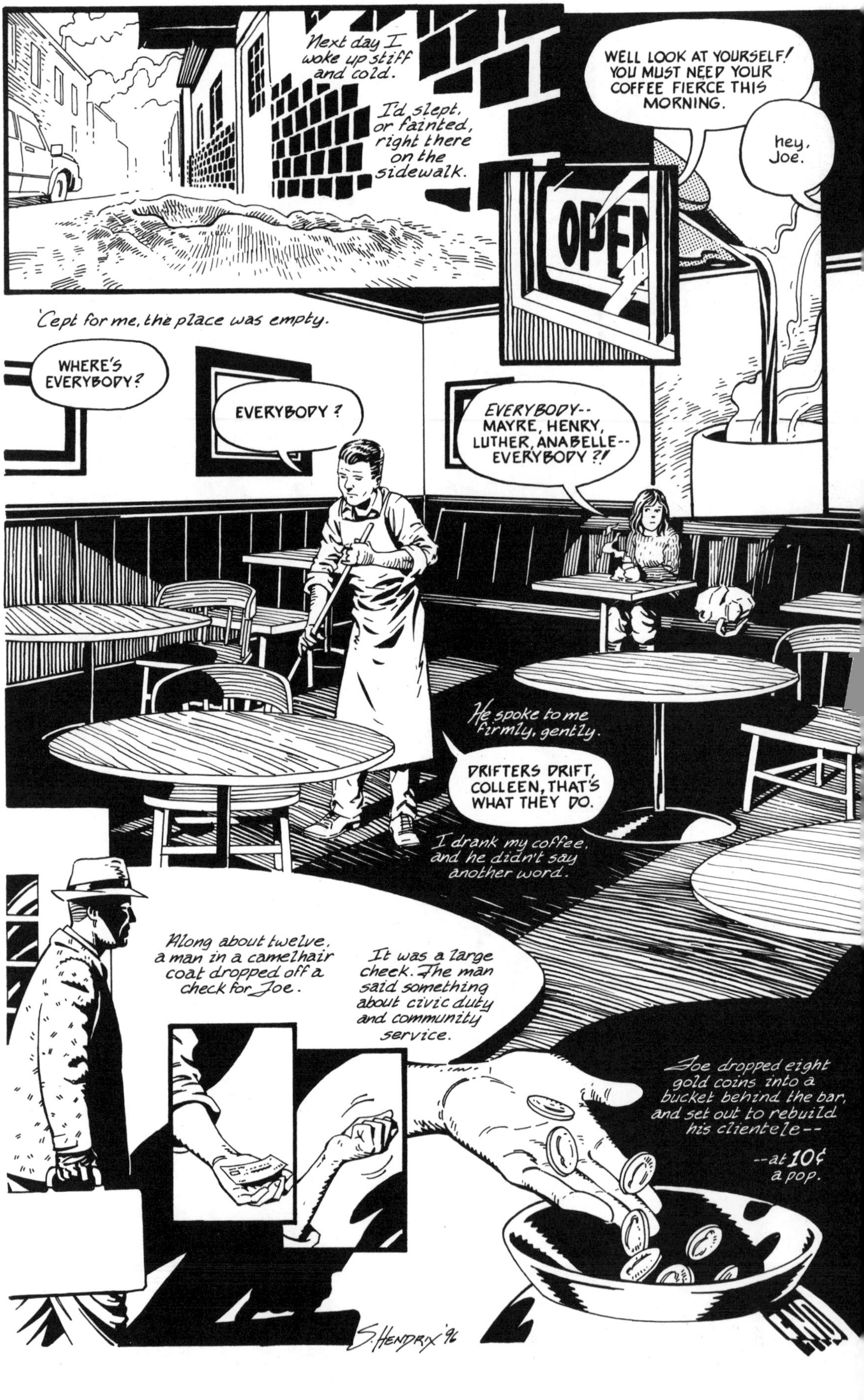
Next day I woke up stiff and cold.
I'd slept, or fainted, right there on the sidewalk.
WELL LOOK AT YOURSELF! YOU MUST NEED YOUR COFFEE FIERCE THIS MORNING.
hey, Joe.
OPEN
'Cept for me, the place was empty.
WHERE'S EVERYBODY?
EVERYBODY ?
EVERYBODY-- MAYRE, HENRY, LUTHER, ANABELLE-- EVERYBODY ?!
He spoke to me firmly, gently.
DRIFTERS DRIFT, COLLEEN, THAT'S WHAT THEY DO.
I drank my coffee, and he didn't say another word.
Along about twelve, a man in a camelhair coat dropped off a check for Joe.
It was a large check. The man said something about civic duty and community service.
Joe dropped eight gold coins into a bucket behind the bar, and set out to rebuild his clientele--
--at 10¢ a pop.
S. HENDRIX '96
END

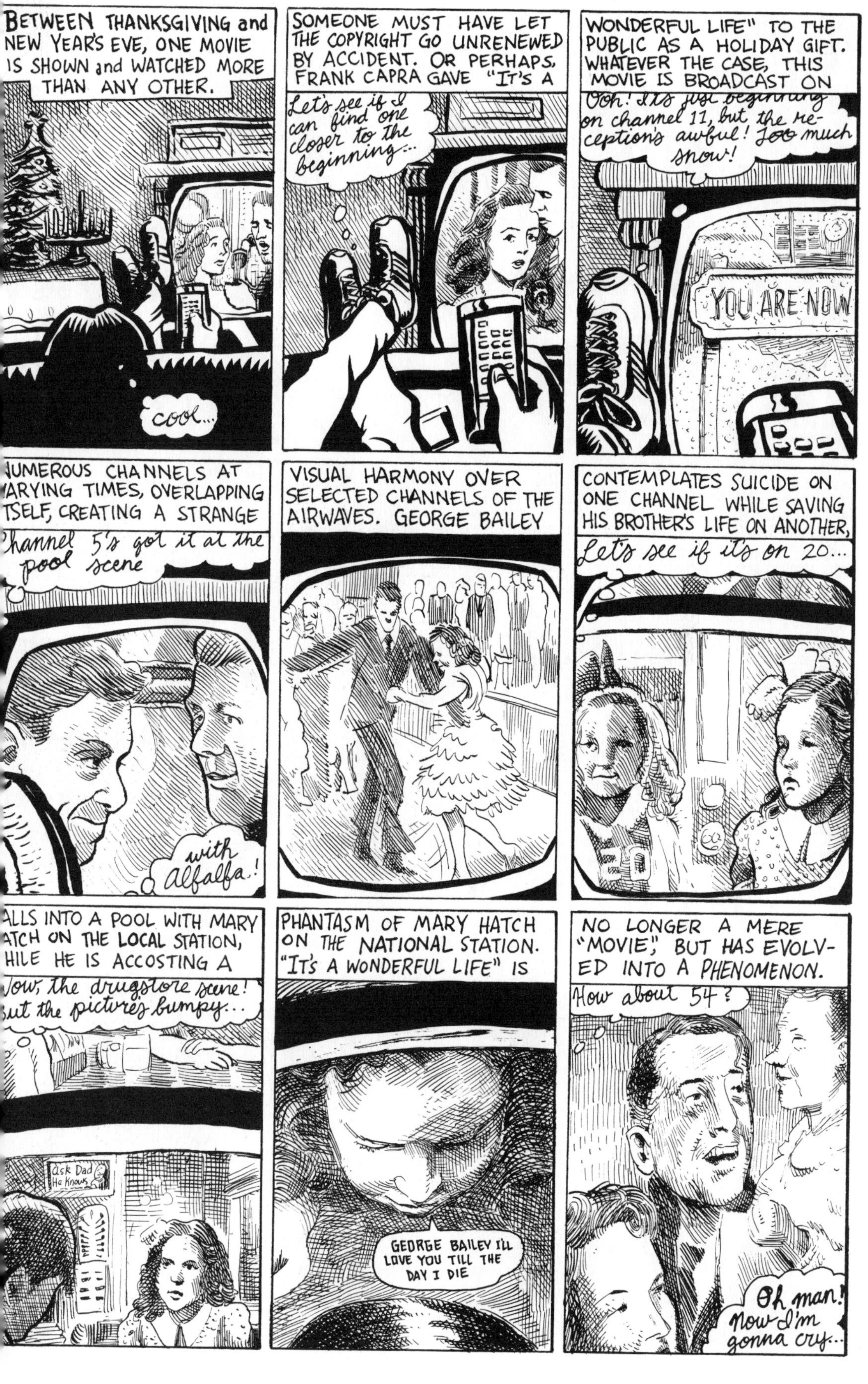

BETWEEN THANKSGIVING and NEW YEAR'S EVE, ONE MOVIE IS SHOWN and WATCHED MORE THAN ANY OTHER.
cool...
SOMEONE MUST HAVE LET THE COPYRIGHT GO UNRENEWED BY ACCIDENT. OR PERHAPS, FRANK CAPRA GAVE "IT'S A
Let's see if I can find one closer to the beginning...
WONDERFUL LIFE" TO THE PUBLIC AS A HOLIDAY GIFT. WHATEVER THE CASE, THIS MOVIE IS BROADCAST ON
Ooh! It's just beginning on channel 11, but the reception's awful! Too much snow!
YOU ARE NOW
NUMEROUS CHANNELS AT VARYING TIMES, OVERLAPPING ITSELF, CREATING A STRANGE
Channel 5's got it at the pool scene
with Alfalfa!
VISUAL HARMONY OVER SELECTED CHANNELS OF THE AIRWAVES. GEORGE BAILEY
CONTEMPLATES SUICIDE ON ONE CHANNEL WHILE SAVING HIS BROTHER'S LIFE ON ANOTHER,
Let's see if it's on 20...
FALLS INTO A POOL WITH MARY HATCH ON THE LOCAL STATION, WHILE HE IS ACCOSTING A
Now, the drugstore scene! But the picture's bumpy...
Ask Dad He Knows
PHANTASM OF MARY HATCH ON THE NATIONAL STATION. "IT'S A WONDERFUL LIFE" IS
GEORGE BAILEY I'LL LOVE YOU TILL THE DAY I DIE
NO LONGER A MERE "MOVIE," BUT HAS EVOLVED INTO A PHENOMENON.
How about 54?
Oh man! Now I'm gonna cry...

You Are Now in Bedford Falls

BY DAVID LASKY

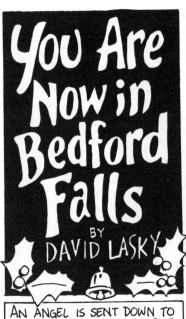

WHAT IS IT ABOUT THIS MOVIE? WHAT CAN ACCOUNT FOR ITS LONGEVITY? WHY DO HOLIDAY VIEWERS WATCH IT REPEATEDLY?

1945 IT STARTED OUT AS A CHRISTMAS CARD~

The Greatest Gift
by Phillip Van Doren

HOLIDAY DEPRESSION IS ONE REASON. IT IS ABOUT A MAN WITH HOLIDAY DEPRESSION. IT IS CHRISTMAS EVE AND HE HAS FAILED HIS FAMILY and COMMUNITY. SO HE DECIDES TO END HIS LIFE...

IT'S A GREAT STORY... UM... A MAN SEES THE WORLD IF HE HAD NEVER EXISTED... UH...

←CAPRA RECRUITING JAMES STEWART→

UH-HUH.

AN ANGEL IS SENT DOWN TO CONVINCE HIM TO RECONSIDER. HIS TACTIC: SHOW THE MAN WHAT THE WORLD WOULD BE LIKE IF HE HADN'T BEEN BORN.

OOH! I'M MAKING IT SOUND AWFUL! IT'S A NICE STORY. I SAW IT ON A CHRISTMAS CARD. I BOUGHT THE RIGHTS FROM R.K.O...

WELL FRANK— I DON'T PICK STORIES, I PICK DIRECTORS... COUNT ME IN!

THE MAN, GEORGE BAILEY, IS HORRIFIED AND REALIZES THAT HE IS A VALUABLE PART of HIS COMMUNITY. HE RUSHES HOME WHERE FAMILY and FRIENDS COME TO HIS AID...

AFTER THE WAR, Y'SEE, I JUST DON'T KNOW IF ACTING IS, IS A-- DECENT THING TO DO...

STEWART WITH LIONEL BARRYMORE

THE MOVIE ACTS AS A WONDERFUL PANACEA TO THOSE WHO FEEL DISAPPOINTED WITH THEMSELVES AROUND THE WINTER HOLIDAYS. BUT IT IS ALSO AN EXTREMELY WELL MADE MOVIE...

IS IT MORE DECENT TO BE DROPPING BOMBS ON PEOPLE?

DIRECTOR FRANK CAPRA SPARED NO EXPENSE IN THE MAKING OF THE MOVIE. HE HAD THE SET OF BEDFORD FALLS BUILT ON THE R.K.O. RANCH AS IF IT WERE AN ACTUAL TOWN. REAL TREES and BUSHES WERE PLANTED.

ENOUGH OF THIS FEELING SORRY FOR YOURSELF. YOU'RE AN ACTOR!

A NEW TYPE of FAKE SNOW WAS DEVELOPED* TO LOOK MORE REAL THAN PAINTED CORN FLAKES. THE SNOW SCENES WERE FILMED IN HOT SOUTHERN CALIFORNIA.

SO ACT! BRING SOME JOY INTO PEOPLE'S LIVES...

RUBBER SKULL CAP→

THANKS LIONEL.

* USING FOAMITE (THE CHEMICAL IN FIRE EXTINGUISHERS), SOAP and WATER.

CAPRA ALSO ASSEMBLED AN EXCELLENT CAST and CREW. JIMMY STEWART STARRED AS GEORGE BAILEY. DONNA REED, GLORIA GRAHAME, LIONEL BARRYMORE, BEULAH BONDI and THOMAS MITCHELL WERE AMONG THE SUPPORTING CAST.

H.B. WARNER, WHO PLAYED MR. GOWER, THE DRUNKEN DRUGGIST, HAD PLAYED CHRIST IN DeMILLE'S "KING OF KINGS" (1927).

I'VE BEEN TYPECAST FOR THE LAST 20 YEARS...

I'LL PLAY A GREAT DRUNK! JUST YOU WAIT!

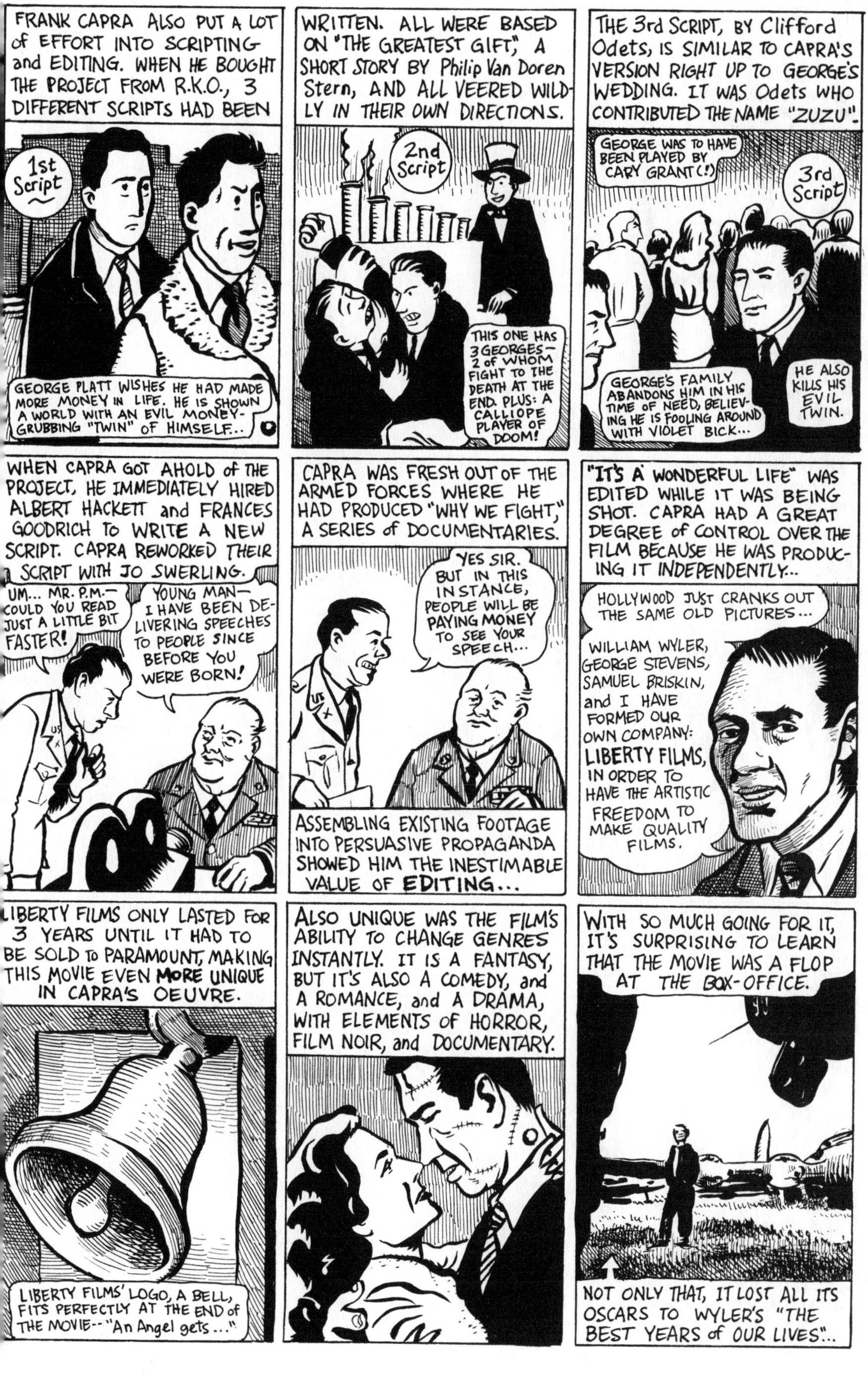
FRANK CAPRA ALSO PUT A LOT of EFFORT INTO SCRIPTING and EDITING. WHEN HE BOUGHT THE PROJECT FROM R.K.O., 3 DIFFERENT SCRIPTS HAD BEEN
1st Script
GEORGE PLATT WISHES HE HAD MADE MORE MONEY IN LIFE. HE IS SHOWN A WORLD WITH AN EVIL MONEY-GRUBBING "TWIN" OF HIMSELF...
WRITTEN. ALL WERE BASED ON "THE GREATEST GIFT," A SHORT STORY BY Philip Van Doren Stern, AND ALL VEERED WILDLY IN THEIR OWN DIRECTIONS.
2nd Script
THIS ONE HAS 3 GEORGES— 2 of WHOM FIGHT TO THE DEATH AT THE END. PLUS: A CALLIOPE PLAYER OF DOOM!
THE 3rd SCRIPT, BY Clifford Odets, IS SIMILAR TO CAPRA'S VERSION RIGHT UP TO GEORGE'S WEDDING. IT WAS Odets WHO CONTRIBUTED THE NAME "ZUZU".
GEORGE WAS TO HAVE BEEN PLAYED BY CARY GRANT (!)
3rd Script
GEORGE'S FAMILY ABANDONS HIM IN HIS TIME OF NEED, BELIEVING HE IS FOOLING AROUND WITH VIOLET BICK...
HE ALSO KILLS HIS EVIL TWIN.
WHEN CAPRA GOT AHOLD of THE PROJECT, HE IMMEDIATELY HIRED ALBERT HACKETT and FRANCES GOODRICH TO WRITE A NEW SCRIPT. CAPRA REWORKED THEIR SCRIPT WITH JO SWERLING.
UM... MR. P.M.— COULD YOU READ JUST A LITTLE BIT FASTER!
YOUNG MAN— I HAVE BEEN DELIVERING SPEECHES TO PEOPLE SINCE BEFORE YOU WERE BORN!
CAPRA WAS FRESH OUT OF THE ARMED FORCES WHERE HE HAD PRODUCED "WHY WE FIGHT," A SERIES of DOCUMENTARIES.
YES SIR. BUT IN THIS INSTANCE, PEOPLE WILL BE PAYING MONEY TO SEE YOUR SPEECH...
ASSEMBLING EXISTING FOOTAGE INTO PERSUASIVE PROPAGANDA SHOWED HIM THE INESTIMABLE VALUE OF EDITING...
"IT'S A WONDERFUL LIFE" WAS EDITED WHILE IT WAS BEING SHOT. CAPRA HAD A GREAT DEGREE of CONTROL OVER THE FILM BECAUSE HE WAS PRODUCING IT INDEPENDENTLY...
HOLLYWOOD JUST CRANKS OUT THE SAME OLD PICTURES...
WILLIAM WYLER, GEORGE STEVENS, SAMUEL BRISKIN, and I HAVE FORMED OUR OWN COMPANY: LIBERTY FILMS, IN ORDER TO HAVE THE ARTISTIC FREEDOM TO MAKE QUALITY FILMS.
LIBERTY FILMS ONLY LASTED FOR 3 YEARS UNTIL IT HAD TO BE SOLD TO PARAMOUNT, MAKING THIS MOVIE EVEN MORE UNIQUE IN CAPRA'S OEUVRE.
LIBERTY FILMS' LOGO, A BELL, FITS PERFECTLY AT THE END of THE MOVIE-- "An Angel gets..."
ALSO UNIQUE WAS THE FILM'S ABILITY TO CHANGE GENRES INSTANTLY. IT IS A FANTASY, BUT IT'S ALSO A COMEDY, and A ROMANCE, and A DRAMA, WITH ELEMENTS of HORROR, FILM NOIR, and DOCUMENTARY.
WITH SO MUCH GOING FOR IT, IT'S SURPRISING TO LEARN THAT THE MOVIE WAS A FLOP AT THE BOX-OFFICE.
NOT ONLY THAT, IT LOST ALL ITS OSCARS TO WYLER'S "THE BEST YEARS of OUR LIVES"...

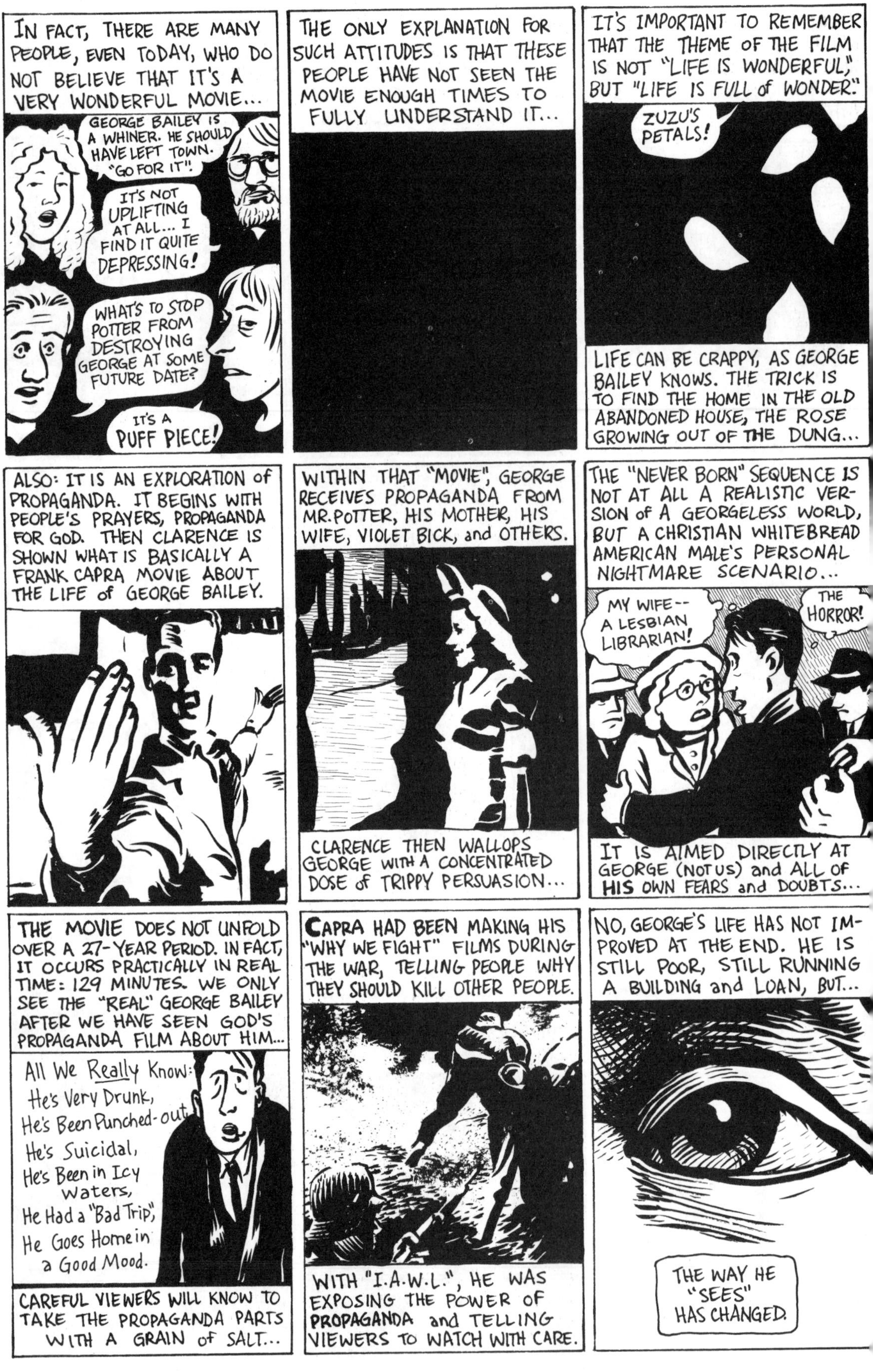
IN FACT, THERE ARE MANY PEOPLE, EVEN TODAY, WHO DO NOT BELIEVE THAT IT'S A VERY WONDERFUL MOVIE...
GEORGE BAILEY IS A WHINER. HE SHOULD HAVE LEFT TOWN. "GO FOR IT"!
IT'S NOT UPLIFTING AT ALL... I FIND IT QUITE DEPRESSING!
WHAT'S TO STOP POTTER FROM DESTROYING GEORGE AT SOME FUTURE DATE?
IT'S A PUFF PIECE!
THE ONLY EXPLANATION FOR SUCH ATTITUDES IS THAT THESE PEOPLE HAVE NOT SEEN THE MOVIE ENOUGH TIMES TO FULLY UNDERSTAND IT...
IT'S IMPORTANT TO REMEMBER THAT THE THEME OF THE FILM IS NOT "LIFE IS WONDERFUL," BUT "LIFE IS FULL of WONDER."
ZUZU'S PETALS!
LIFE CAN BE CRAPPY, AS GEORGE BAILEY KNOWS. THE TRICK IS TO FIND THE HOME IN THE OLD ABANDONED HOUSE, THE ROSE GROWING OUT OF THE DUNG...
ALSO: IT IS AN EXPLORATION of PROPAGANDA. IT BEGINS WITH PEOPLE'S PRAYERS, PROPAGANDA FOR GOD. THEN CLARENCE IS SHOWN WHAT IS BASICALLY A FRANK CAPRA MOVIE ABOUT THE LIFE of GEORGE BAILEY.
WITHIN THAT "MOVIE", GEORGE RECEIVES PROPAGANDA FROM MR. POTTER, HIS MOTHER, HIS WIFE, VIOLET BICK, and OTHERS.
CLARENCE THEN WALLOPS GEORGE WITH A CONCENTRATED DOSE of TRIPPY PERSUASION...
THE "NEVER BORN" SEQUENCE IS NOT AT ALL A REALISTIC VERSION of A GEORGELESS WORLD, BUT A CHRISTIAN WHITEBREAD AMERICAN MALE'S PERSONAL NIGHTMARE SCENARIO...
MY WIFE-- A LESBIAN LIBRARIAN!
THE HORROR!
IT IS AIMED DIRECTLY AT GEORGE (NOT US) and ALL OF HIS OWN FEARS and DOUBTS...
THE MOVIE DOES NOT UNFOLD OVER A 27-YEAR PERIOD. IN FACT, IT OCCURS PRACTICALLY IN REAL TIME: 129 MINUTES. WE ONLY SEE THE "REAL" GEORGE BAILEY AFTER WE HAVE SEEN GOD'S PROPAGANDA FILM ABOUT HIM...
All We Really Know:
He's Very Drunk,
He's Been Punched-out
He's Suicidal,
He's Been in Icy Waters,
He Had a "Bad Trip,"
He Goes Home in a Good Mood.
CAREFUL VIEWERS WILL KNOW TO TAKE THE PROPAGANDA PARTS WITH A GRAIN of SALT...
CAPRA HAD BEEN MAKING HIS "WHY WE FIGHT" FILMS DURING THE WAR, TELLING PEOPLE WHY THEY SHOULD KILL OTHER PEOPLE.
WITH "I.A.W.L.", HE WAS EXPOSING THE POWER OF PROPAGANDA and TELLING VIEWERS TO WATCH WITH CARE.
NO, GEORGE'S LIFE HAS NOT IMPROVED AT THE END. HE IS STILL POOR, STILL RUNNING A BUILDING and LOAN, BUT...
THE WAY HE "SEES" HAS CHANGED.

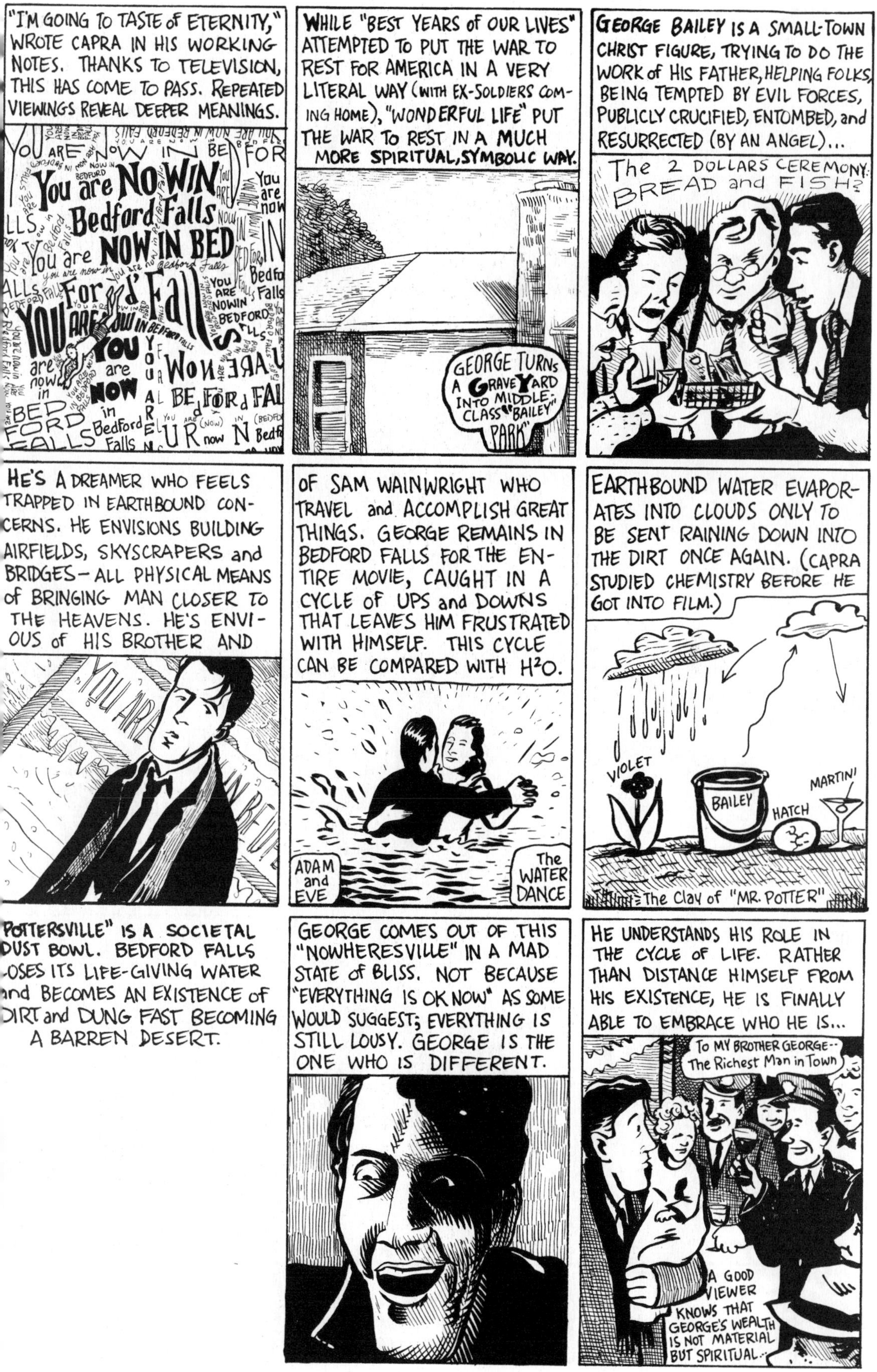
"I'M GOING TO TASTE OF ETERNITY," WROTE CAPRA IN HIS WORKING NOTES. THANKS TO TELEVISION, THIS HAS COME TO PASS. REPEATED VIEWINGS REVEAL DEEPER MEANINGS.
You are NOWIN Bedford Falls NOW IN BED
YOU ARE NOW IN BEDFORD FALLS
You are now in Bedford Falls
WHILE "BEST YEARS OF OUR LIVES" ATTEMPTED TO PUT THE WAR TO REST FOR AMERICA IN A VERY LITERAL WAY (WITH EX-SOLDIERS COMING HOME), "WONDERFUL LIFE" PUT THE WAR TO REST IN A MUCH MORE SPIRITUAL, SYMBOLIC WAY.
GEORGE TURNS A GRAVEYARD INTO MIDDLE-CLASS "BAILEY" PARK
GEORGE BAILEY IS A SMALL-TOWN CHRIST FIGURE, TRYING TO DO THE WORK OF HIS FATHER, HELPING FOLKS, BEING TEMPTED BY EVIL FORCES, PUBLICLY CRUCIFIED, ENTOMBED, and RESURRECTED (BY AN ANGEL)...
The 2 DOLLARS CEREMONY: BREAD and FISH?
HE'S A DREAMER WHO FEELS TRAPPED IN EARTHBOUND CONCERNS. HE ENVISIONS BUILDING AIRFIELDS, SKYSCRAPERS and BRIDGES — ALL PHYSICAL MEANS of BRINGING MAN CLOSER TO THE HEAVENS. HE'S ENVIOUS of HIS BROTHER AND
YOU ARE
OF SAM WAINWRIGHT WHO TRAVEL and ACCOMPLISH GREAT THINGS. GEORGE REMAINS IN BEDFORD FALLS FOR THE ENTIRE MOVIE, CAUGHT IN A CYCLE of UPS and DOWNS THAT LEAVES HIM FRUSTRATED WITH HIMSELF. THIS CYCLE CAN BE COMPARED WITH H^2O.
ADAM and EVE
The WATER DANCE
EARTHBOUND WATER EVAPORATES INTO CLOUDS ONLY TO BE SENT RAINING DOWN INTO THE DIRT ONCE AGAIN. (CAPRA STUDIED CHEMISTRY BEFORE HE GOT INTO FILM.)
VIOLET
BAILEY
HATCH
MARTINI
The Clay of "MR. POTTER"
POTTERSVILLE" IS A SOCIETAL DUST BOWL. BEDFORD FALLS LOSES ITS LIFE-GIVING WATER and BECOMES AN EXISTENCE of DIRT and DUNG FAST BECOMING A BARREN DESERT.
GEORGE COMES OUT OF THIS "NOWHERESVILLE" IN A MAD STATE of BLISS. NOT BECAUSE "EVERYTHING IS OK NOW" AS SOME WOULD SUGGEST; EVERYTHING IS STILL LOUSY. GEORGE IS THE ONE WHO IS DIFFERENT.
HE UNDERSTANDS HIS ROLE IN THE CYCLE of LIFE. RATHER THAN DISTANCE HIMSELF FROM HIS EXISTENCE, HE IS FINALLY ABLE TO EMBRACE WHO HE IS...
To MY BROTHER GEORGE -- The Richest Man in Town
A GOOD VIEWER KNOWS THAT GEORGE'S WEALTH IS NOT MATERIAL BUT SPIRITUAL...

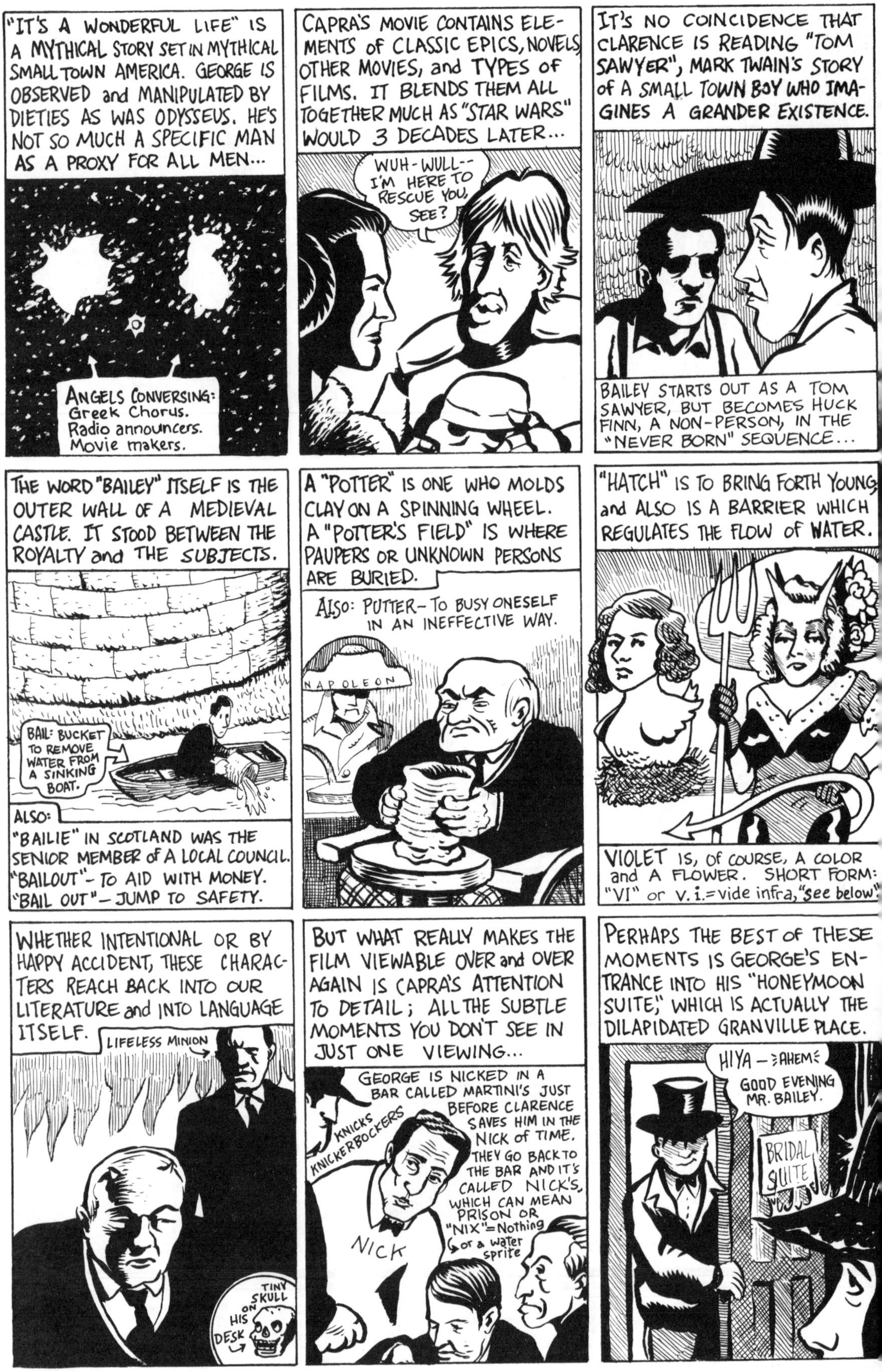

"IT'S A WONDERFUL LIFE" IS A MYTHICAL STORY SET IN MYTHICAL SMALL TOWN AMERICA. GEORGE IS OBSERVED and MANIPULATED BY DIETIES AS WAS ODYSSEUS. HE'S NOT SO MUCH A SPECIFIC MAN AS A PROXY FOR ALL MEN...
ANGELS CONVERSING: Greek Chorus. Radio announcers. Movie makers.
CAPRA'S MOVIE CONTAINS ELEMENTS of CLASSIC EPICS, NOVELS, OTHER MOVIES, and TYPES of FILMS. IT BLENDS THEM ALL TOGETHER MUCH AS "STAR WARS" WOULD 3 DECADES LATER...
WUH-WULL-- I'M HERE TO RESCUE YOU, SEE?
IT'S NO COINCIDENCE THAT CLARENCE IS READING "TOM SAWYER", MARK TWAIN'S STORY of A SMALL TOWN BOY WHO IMAGINES A GRANDER EXISTENCE.
BAILEY STARTS OUT AS A TOM SAWYER, BUT BECOMES HUCK FINN, A NON-PERSON, IN THE "NEVER BORN" SEQUENCE...
THE WORD "BAILEY" ITSELF IS THE OUTER WALL OF A MEDIEVAL CASTLE. IT STOOD BETWEEN THE ROYALTY and THE SUBJECTS.
BAIL: BUCKET TO REMOVE WATER FROM A SINKING BOAT.
ALSO:
"BAILIE" IN SCOTLAND WAS THE SENIOR MEMBER of A LOCAL COUNCIL. "BAILOUT" - TO AID WITH MONEY. "BAIL OUT" - JUMP TO SAFETY.
A "POTTER" IS ONE WHO MOLDS CLAY ON A SPINNING WHEEL. A "POTTER'S FIELD" IS WHERE PAUPERS OR UNKNOWN PERSONS ARE BURIED.
ALSO: PUTTER - TO BUSY ONESELF IN AN INEFFECTIVE WAY.
NAPOLEON
"HATCH" IS TO BRING FORTH YOUNG, and ALSO IS A BARRIER WHICH REGULATES THE FLOW of WATER.
VIOLET IS, of COURSE, A COLOR and A FLOWER. SHORT FORM: "VI" or v. i. = vide infra, "see below"
WHETHER INTENTIONAL OR BY HAPPY ACCIDENT, THESE CHARACTERS REACH BACK INTO OUR LITERATURE and INTO LANGUAGE ITSELF.
LIFELESS MINION
TINY SKULL ON HIS DESK
BUT WHAT REALLY MAKES THE FILM VIEWABLE OVER and OVER AGAIN IS CAPRA'S ATTENTION TO DETAIL; ALL THE SUBTLE MOMENTS YOU DON'T SEE IN JUST ONE VIEWING...
GEORGE IS NICKED IN A BAR CALLED MARTINI'S JUST BEFORE CLARENCE SAVES HIM IN THE NICK of TIME. THEY GO BACK TO THE BAR AND IT'S CALLED NICK'S, WHICH CAN MEAN PRISON OR "NIX" = Nothing or a water sprite
KNICKS KNICKERBOCKERS
NICK
PERHAPS THE BEST of THESE MOMENTS IS GEORGE'S ENTRANCE INTO HIS "HONEYMOON SUITE," WHICH IS ACTUALLY THE DILAPIDATED GRANVILLE PLACE.
HIYA - AHEM - GOOD EVENING MR. BAILEY.
BRIDAL SUITE

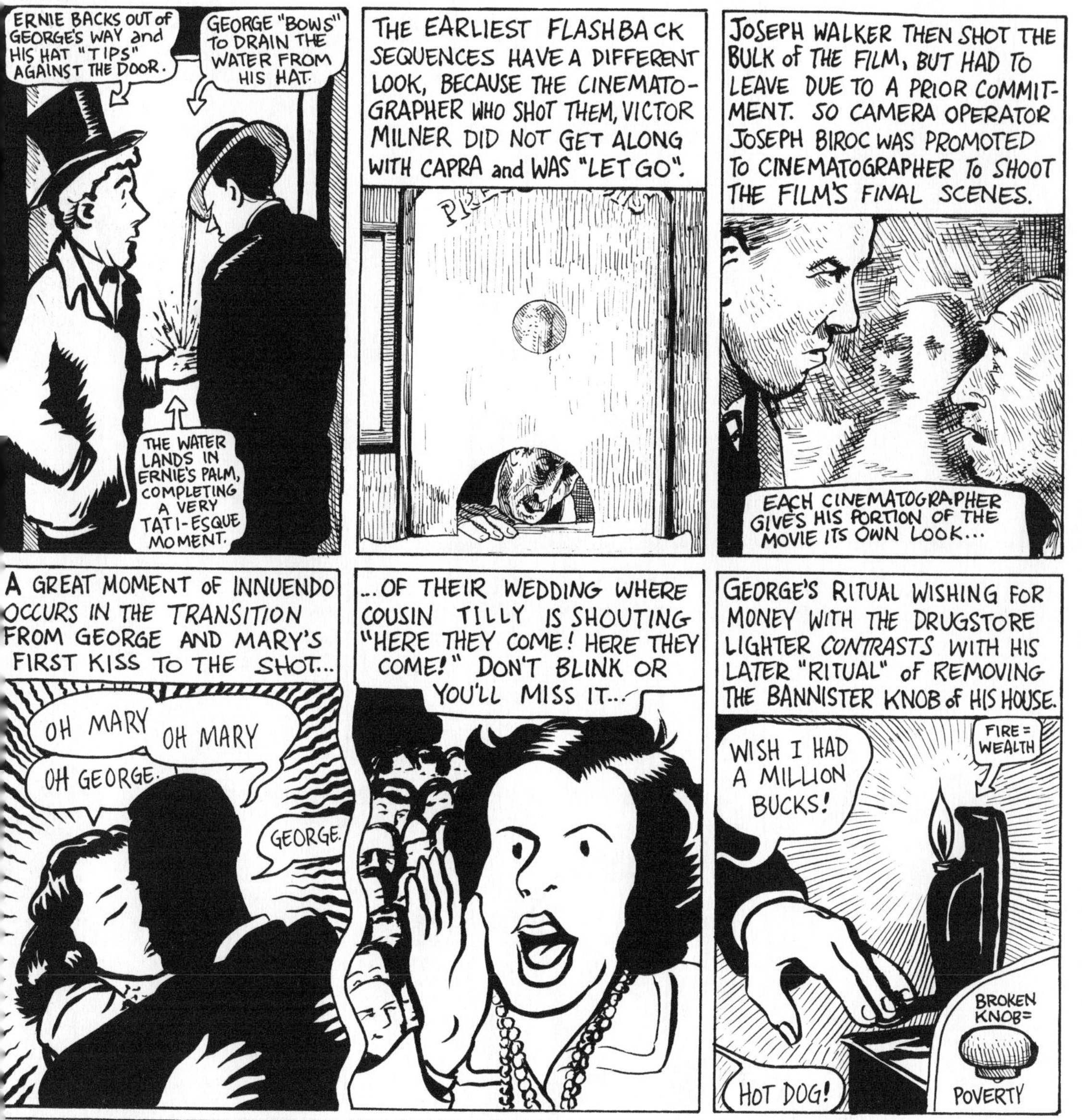
ERNIE BACKS OUT of GEORGE'S WAY and HIS HAT "TIPS" AGAINST THE DOOR.
GEORGE "BOWS" TO DRAIN THE WATER FROM HIS HAT.
THE WATER LANDS IN ERNIE'S PALM, COMPLETING A VERY TATI-ESQUE MOMENT.
THE EARLIEST FLASHBACK SEQUENCES HAVE A DIFFERENT LOOK, BECAUSE THE CINEMATOGRAPHER WHO SHOT THEM, VICTOR MILNER DID NOT GET ALONG WITH CAPRA and WAS "LET GO".
JOSEPH WALKER THEN SHOT THE BULK of THE FILM, BUT HAD TO LEAVE DUE TO A PRIOR COMMITMENT. SO CAMERA OPERATOR JOSEPH BIROC WAS PROMOTED TO CINEMATOGRAPHER TO SHOOT THE FILM'S FINAL SCENES.
EACH CINEMATOGRAPHER GIVES HIS PORTION OF THE MOVIE ITS OWN LOOK...
A GREAT MOMENT OF INNUENDO OCCURS IN THE TRANSITION FROM GEORGE AND MARY'S FIRST KISS TO THE SHOT...
OH MARY
OH MARY
OH GEORGE.
GEORGE.
...OF THEIR WEDDING WHERE COUSIN TILLY IS SHOUTING "HERE THEY COME! HERE THEY COME!" DON'T BLINK OR YOU'LL MISS IT...
GEORGE'S RITUAL WISHING FOR MONEY WITH THE DRUGSTORE LIGHTER CONTRASTS WITH HIS LATER "RITUAL" of REMOVING THE BANNISTER KNOB of HIS HOUSE.
WISH I HAD A MILLION BUCKS!
FIRE= WEALTH
HOT DOG!
BROKEN KNOB=
POVERTY
CAPRA WAS OFTEN WILLING O IMPROVISE. IN THE BANK-RUN SCENE, HE DIDN'T TELL STEWART HOW MUCH ELLEN CORBY WOULD ASK FOR... TEWART'S KISS IS SPONTANEOUS.
COULD I HAVE SEVENTEEN FIFTY?
CORBY WOULD LATER APPEAR OPPOSITE STEWART IN "Vertigo".
JIMMY THE RAVEN WAS A LAST-MINUTE ADDITION TO THE CAST. HE LOOMS SYMBOLICALLY OVER A MODEL HOME AS GEORGE IS ABOUT TO LEAVE THE BUILDING and LOAN.
NEVERMORE
THEY'LL VOTE WITH POTTER OTHERWISE!
ACTORS' VOICES FALTER AT JUST THE RIGHT MOMENTS.
THE PERFECT PET FOR MAD UNCLE BILLY.
WHEN CLARENCE IS FIRST SHOWN, HE IS NOT INTRODUCED IN ANY WAY. JOSEPH THE ANGEL IS NO LONGER NARRATING FOR US. WE ARE IN "REAL TIME".
THE ODD CUT THAT RESULTS COULD NEVER HAVE HAPPENED IN A SLICK STUDIO PRODUCTION...

"IT'S A WONDERFUL LIFE" NOT ONLY CELEBRATES HUMAN IMAGINATION, IT TURNS ON THE IMAGINATIONS OF THE VIEWERS WATCHING IT...

Jimmy Stewart was a bomber pilot in the war with over 2,000 hours in the air.

IN THE VAGUE "RADIO PLAY" STYLE PRESENTATION OF HEAVEN, EVERY VIEWER IS ALLOWED TO IMAGINE THEIR OWN TYPE of HEAVEN.

A successful actor and decorated war hero, he was in real life everything that George Bailey could not be...

MARY'S FLINCHES ALLOW THE VIEWER TO IMAGINE GOWER'S BLOWS TO BE WORSE THAN ANYTHING CAPRA COULD ACTUALLY SHOW.

Frank Capra immigrated with his family from Sicily at age six.

WE ARE ONLY SHOWN SMALL SELECTIONS FROM GEORGE'S LIFE...

They settled in Los Angeles.

Like George Bailey, he never really left his home town.

In 1928, he got a job directing for Columbia Pictures.

...BUT IT IS ENOUGH FOR OUR IMAGINATIONS TO FILL IN THE DETAILS...

His triumphs were often followed by tragedies. Not long after winning a college scholarship, he learned that his father had died.

He lost his young son on the day that "You can't take it with you" was previewed.

THE ULTIMATE MESSAGE OF THE FILM, THE ONE THAT CAPRA SPELLS OUT FOR US, IS A CELEBRATION OF FRIENDS and FAMILY...

The initial failure of "Wonderful Life" dampened Capra's creative spirits.

He had always wrestled with self-doubt.

He ended his career as a lecturer and producer of educational films.

LIFE'S GREATEST CHALLENGE IS IN THE BRIDGING OF IMAGINATION and REALITY IN THE FORMS OF A FAMILY and A COMMUNITY...

But he did live to see "I.A.W.L." become a Holiday Phenomenon.

...THESE ARE ALSO LIFE'S GREATEST SUCCESSES.

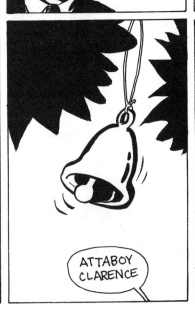

ATTABOY CLARENCE

FURTHER READING:

"FRANK CAPRA" by Charles J. Maland

THE IT'S A WONDERFUL LIFE Book by Jeanine Basinger

"AMERICAN VISION" by Raymond Carney

Thanks to: Jim Woodring William S. Blackwell David E. Lasky Ivan Brunetti and everyone else who has been willing to discuss this movie with me...

WHERE THE ELVES COME FROM

STORY BY CHARLIE WISE · ART BY DAVID LEE INGERSOLL

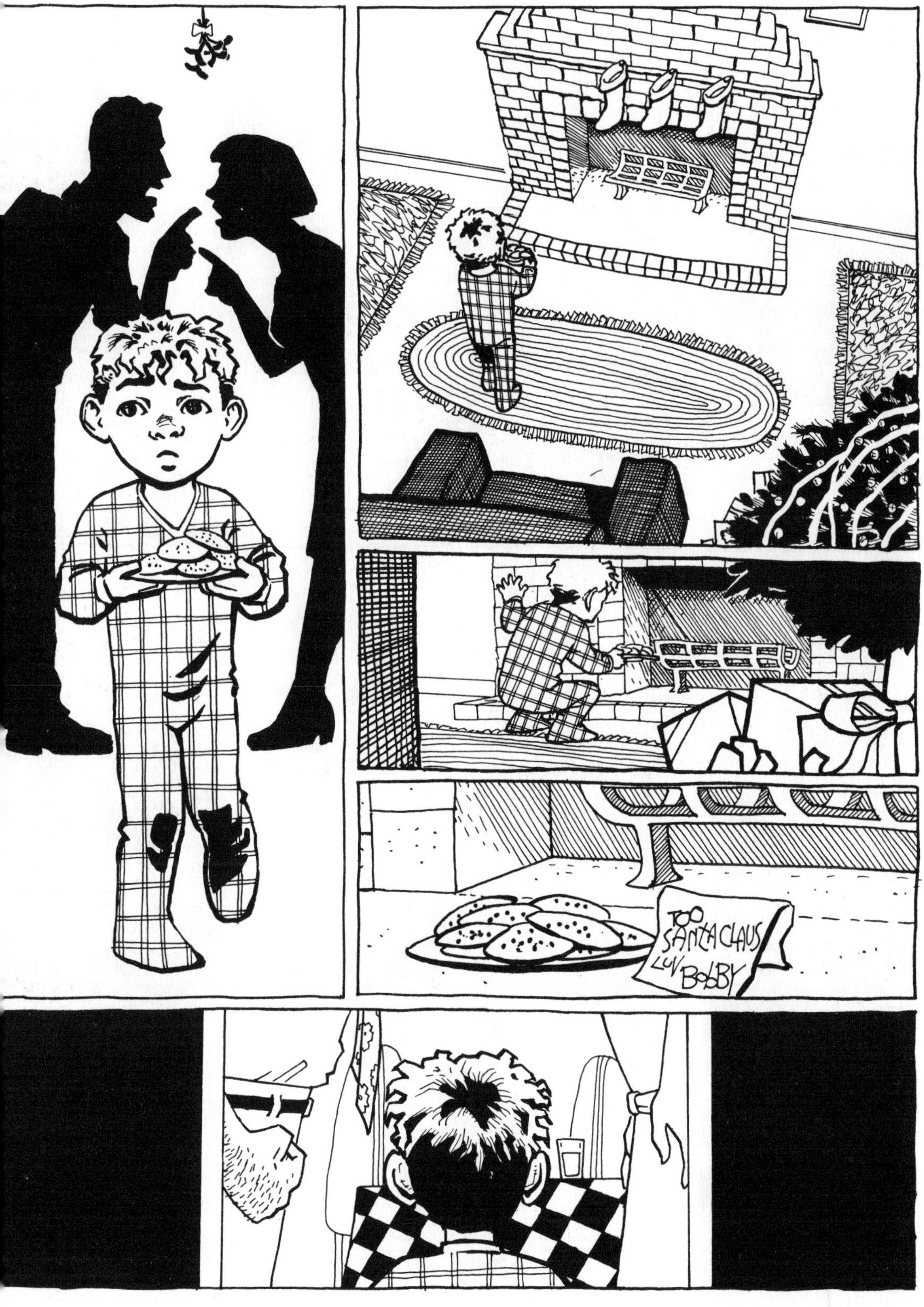
TO SANTA CLAUS
LUV BOBBY

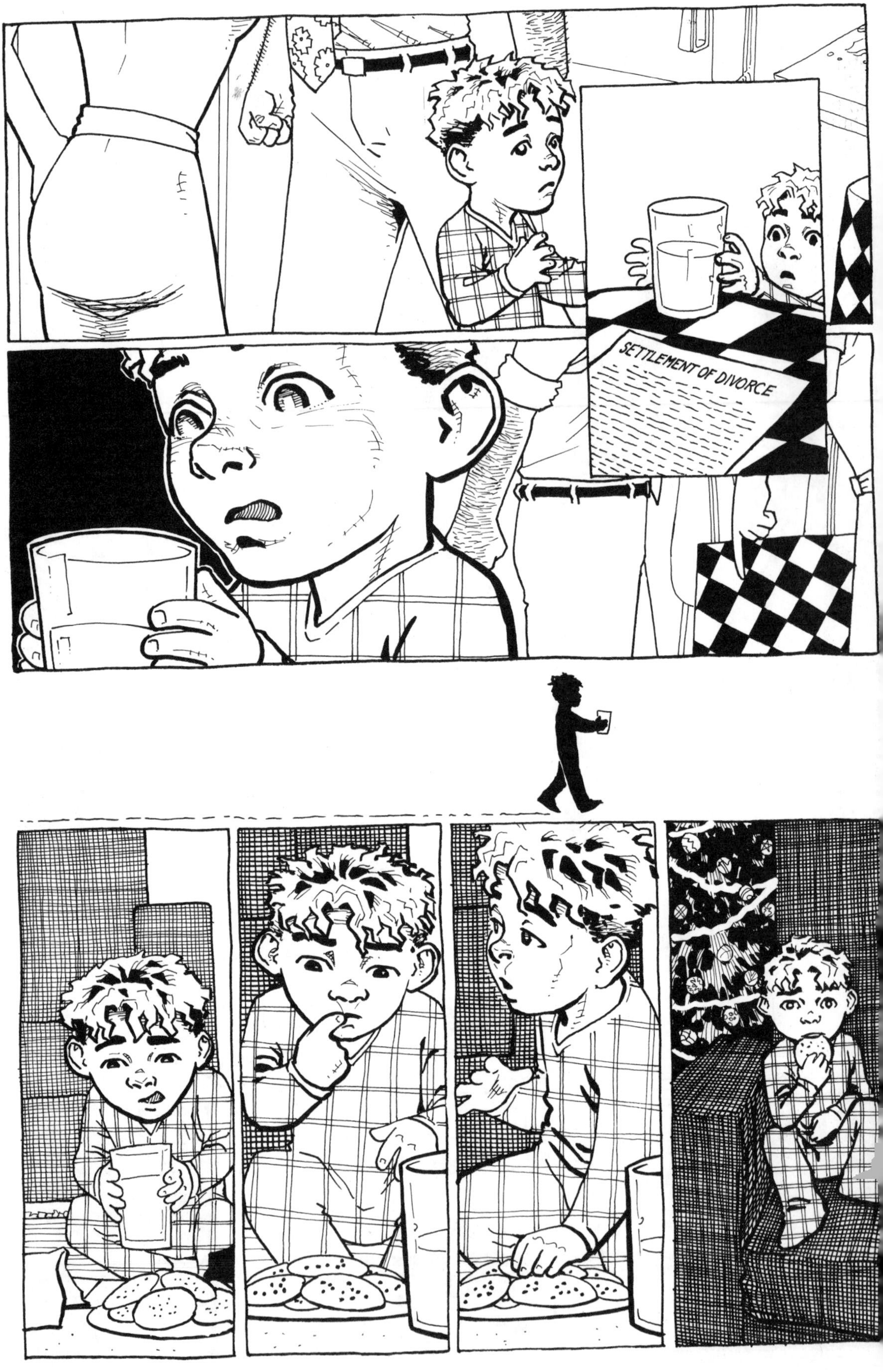
SETTLEMENT OF DIVORCE

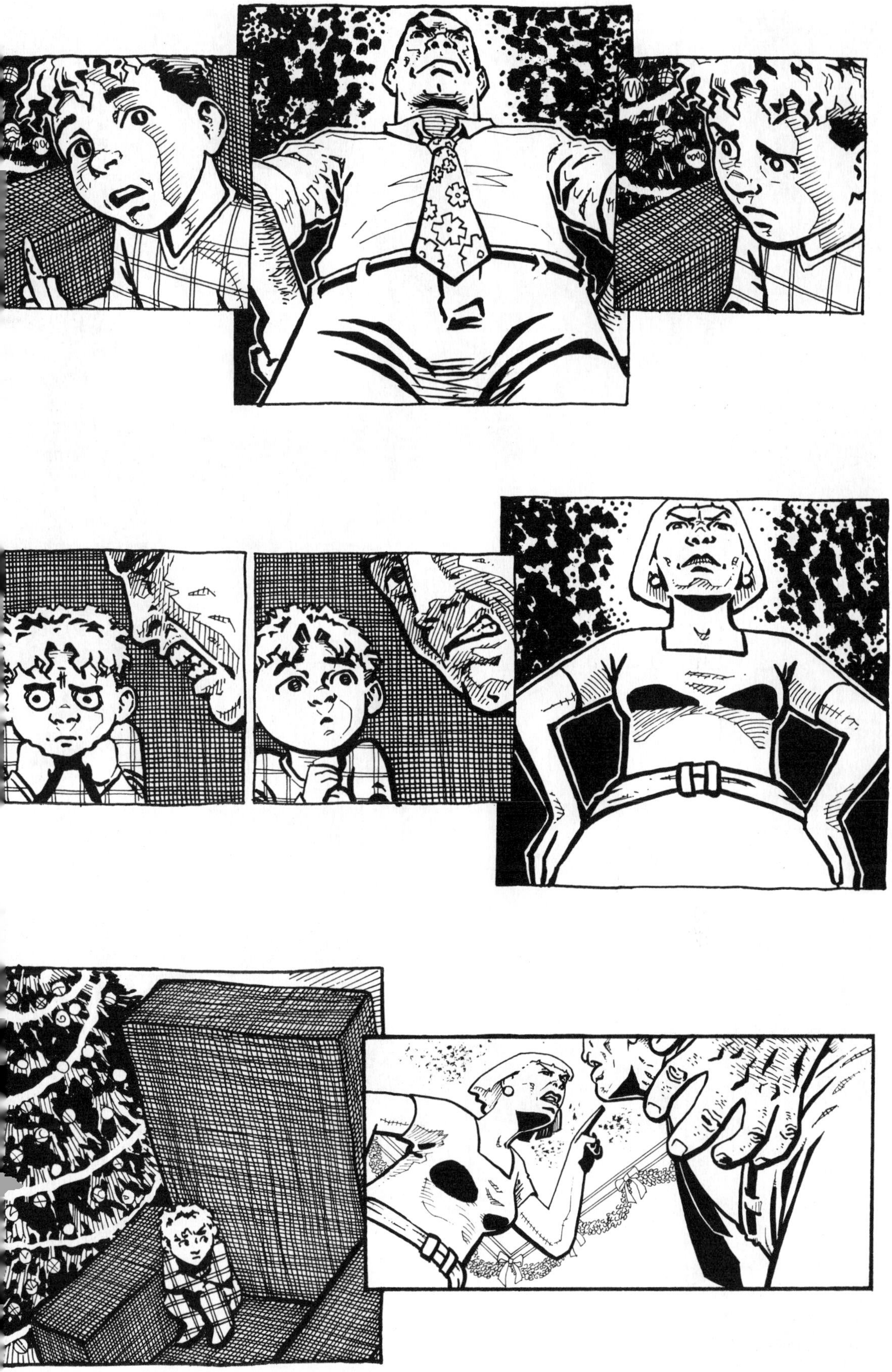

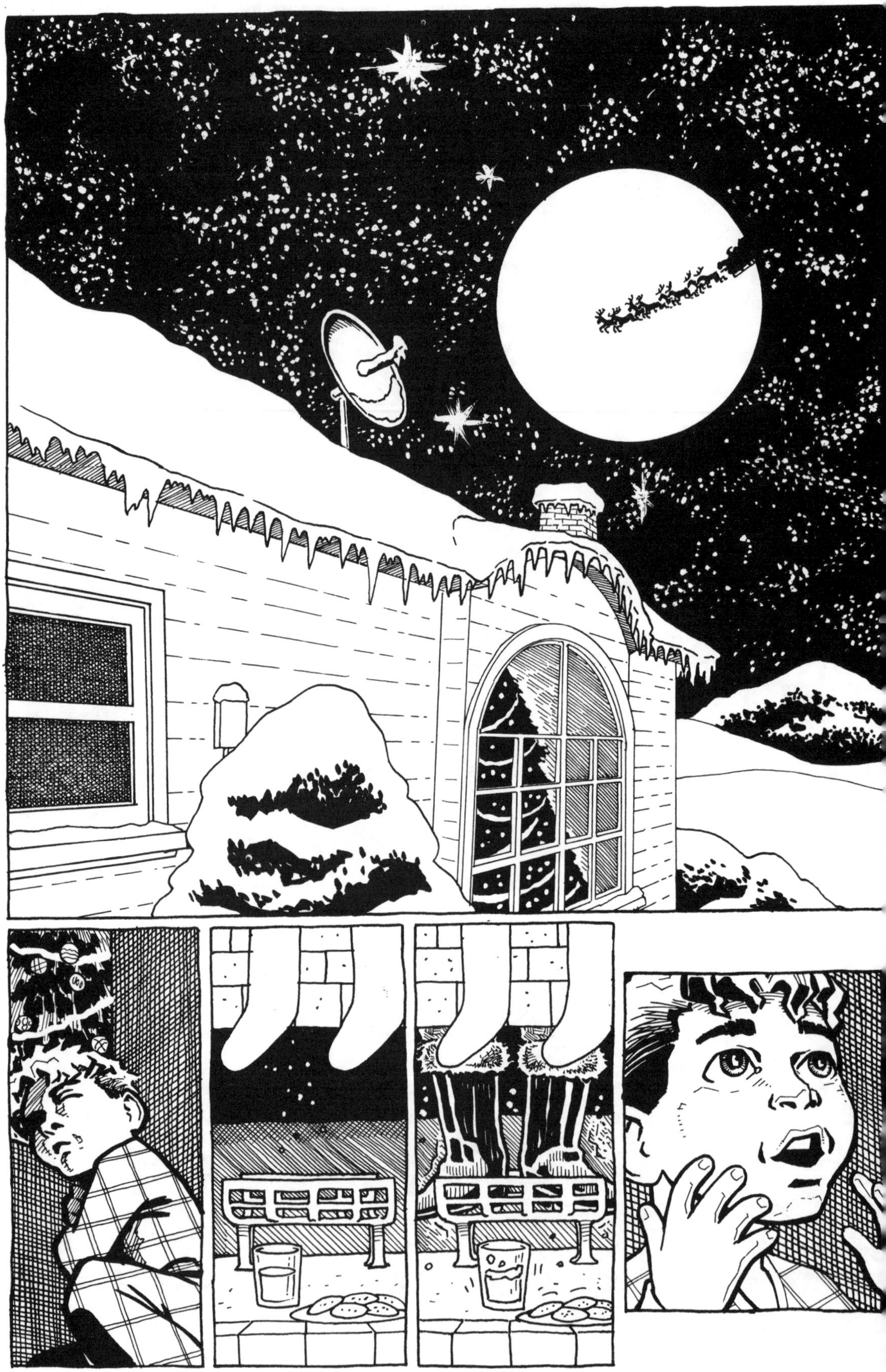

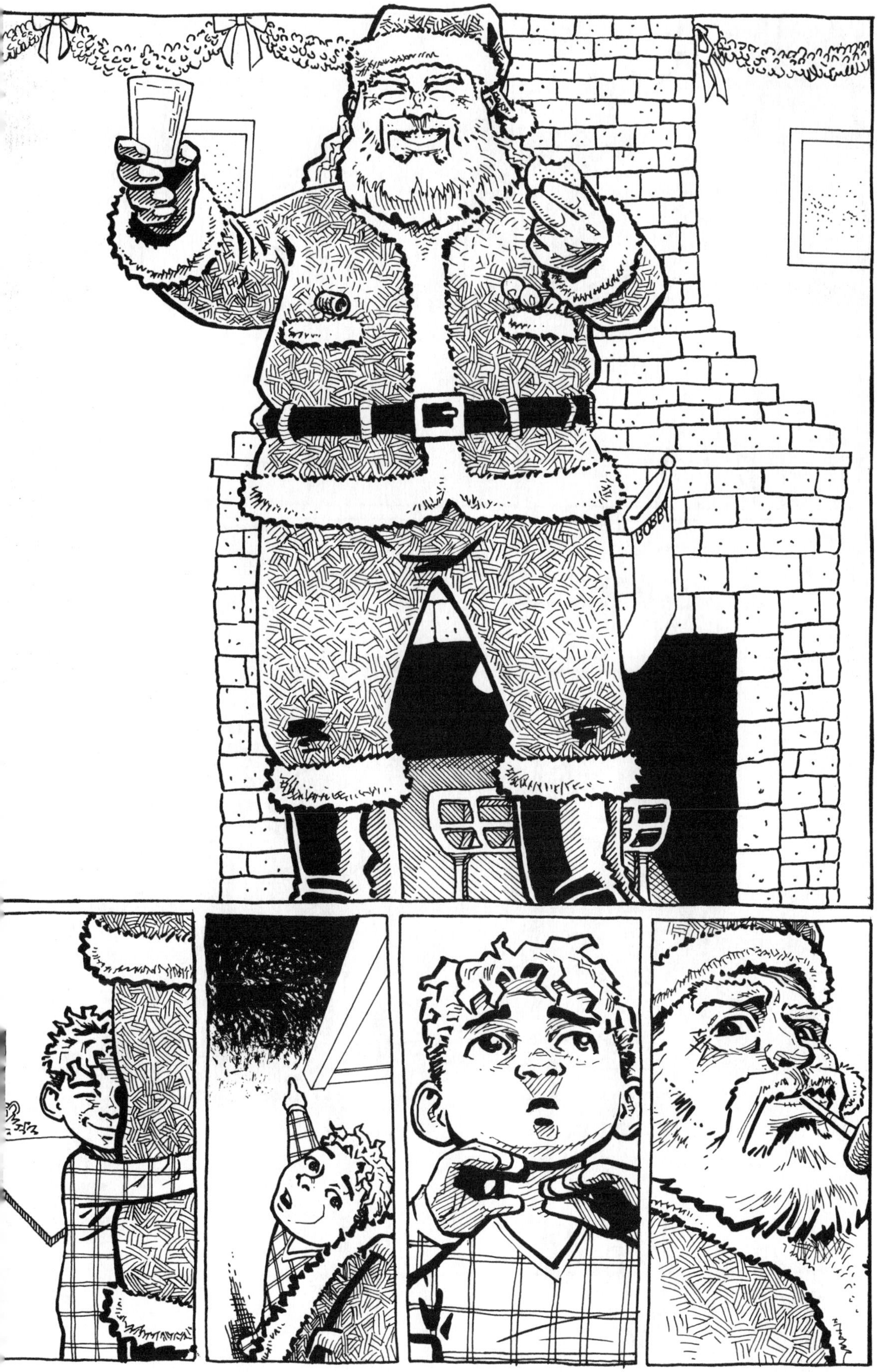
BOBBY

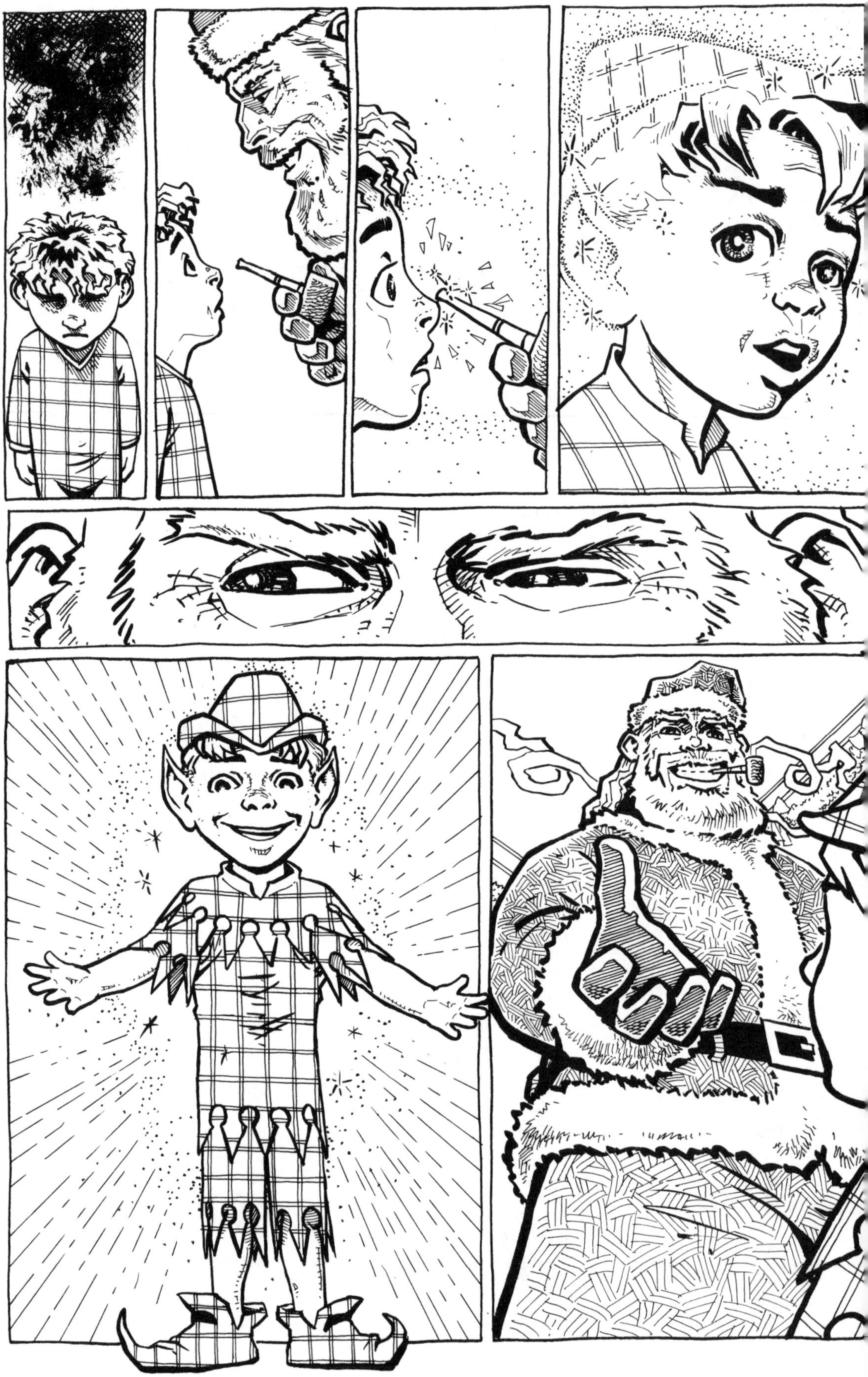

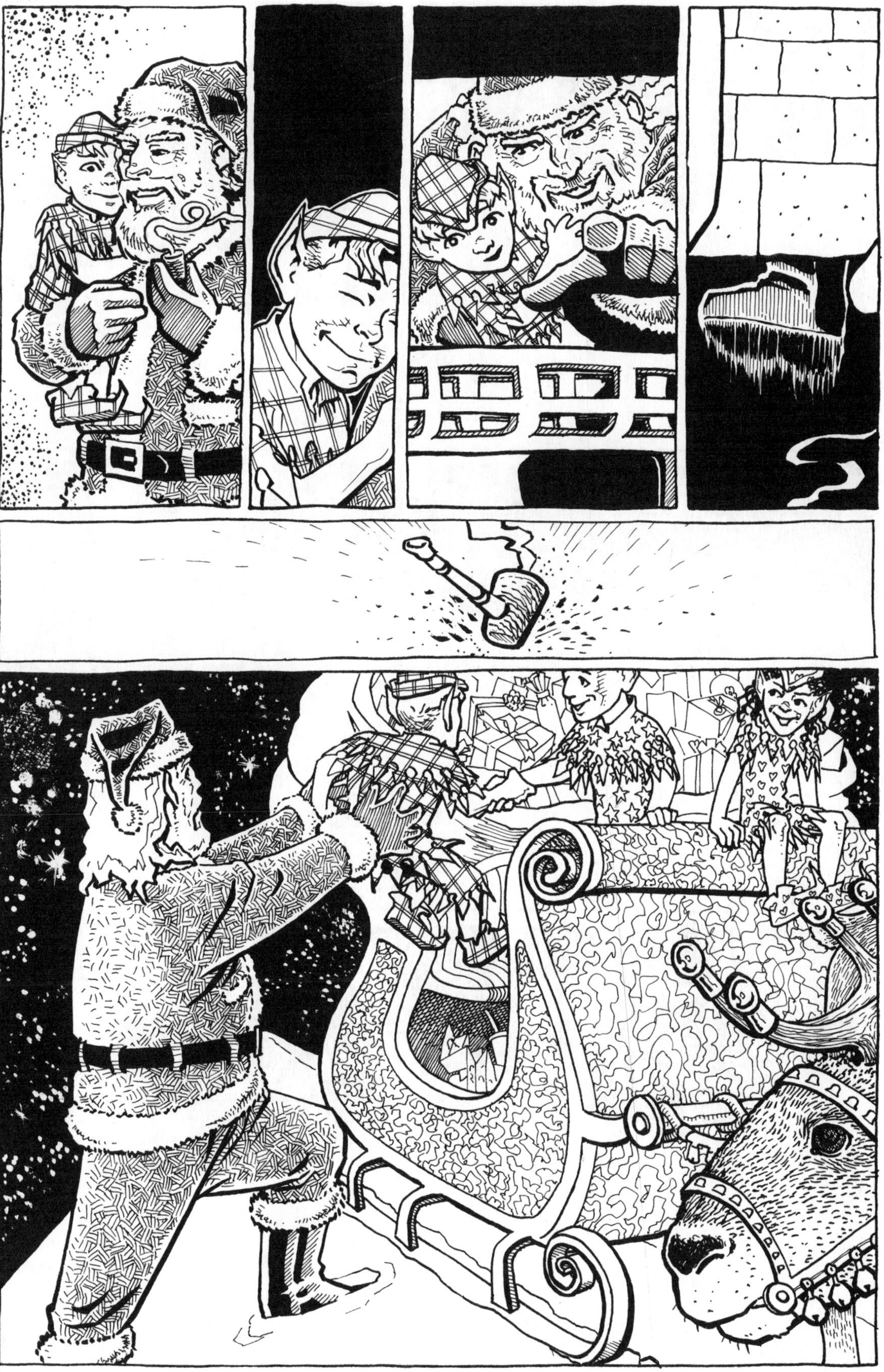

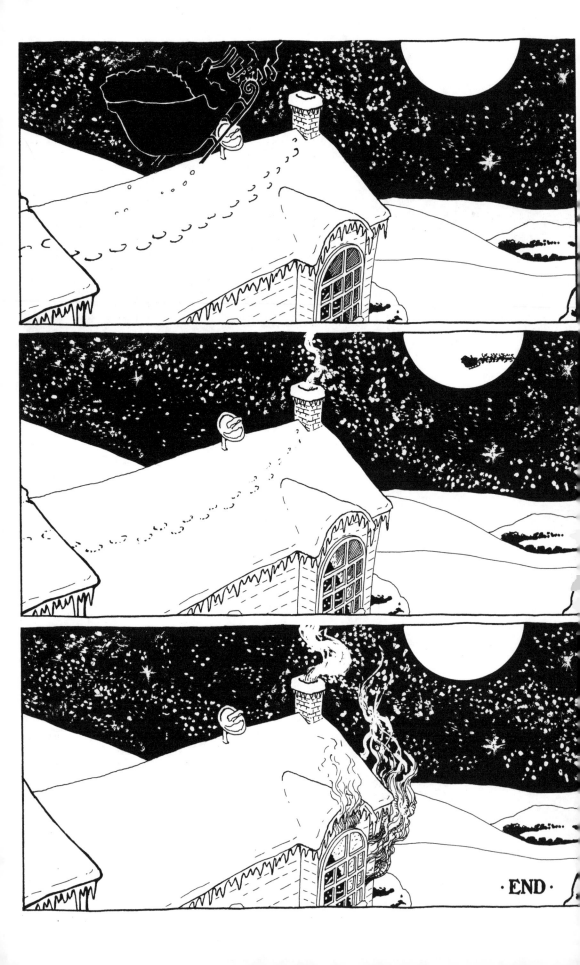

· END ·

WHITE CHRISTMAS

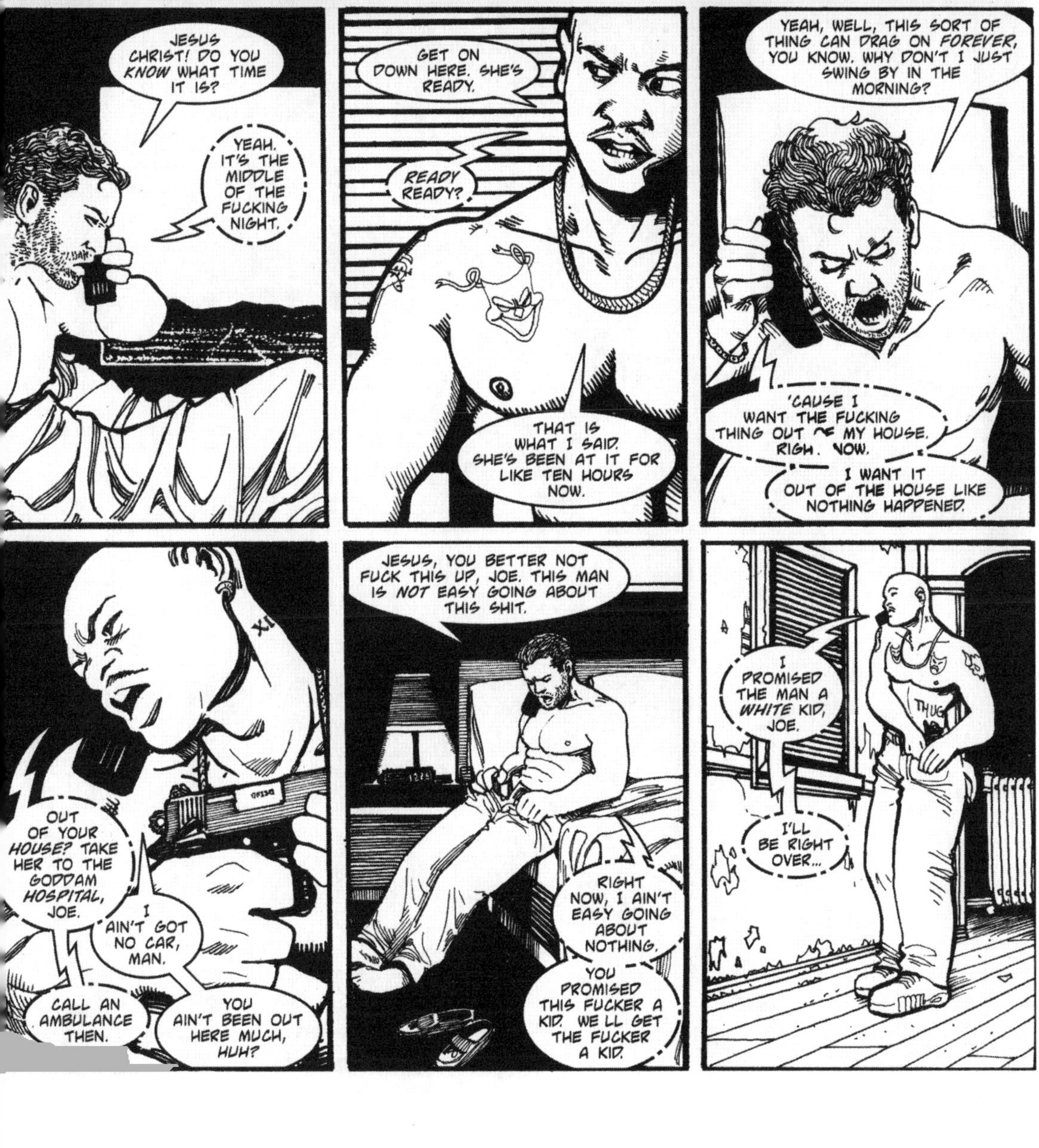
JESUS CHRIST! DO YOU *KNOW* WHAT TIME IT IS?
YEAH. IT'S THE MIDDLE OF THE FUCKING NIGHT.
GET ON DOWN HERE. SHE'S READY.
READY READY?
THAT IS WHAT I SAID. SHE'S BEEN AT IT FOR LIKE TEN HOURS NOW.
YEAH, WELL, THIS SORT OF THING CAN DRAG ON *FOREVER*, YOU KNOW. WHY DON'T I JUST SWING BY IN THE MORNING?
'CAUSE I WANT THE FUCKING THING OUT MY HOUSE. RIGH NOW.
I WANT IT OUT OF THE HOUSE LIKE NOTHING HAPPENED.
OUT OF YOUR *HOUSE?* TAKE HER TO THE GODDAM *HOSPITAL*, JOE.
I AIN'T GOT NO CAR, MAN.
CALL AN AMBULANCE THEN.
YOU AIN'T BEEN OUT HERE MUCH, *HUH?*
JESUS, YOU BETTER NOT FUCK THIS UP, JOE. THIS MAN IS *NOT* EASY GOING ABOUT THIS SHIT.
RIGHT NOW, I AIN'T EASY GOING ABOUT NOTHING.
YOU PROMISED THIS FUCKER A KID. WE LL GET THE FUCKER A KID.
I PROMISED THE MAN A *WHITE* KID, JOE.
I'LL BE RIGHT OVER...

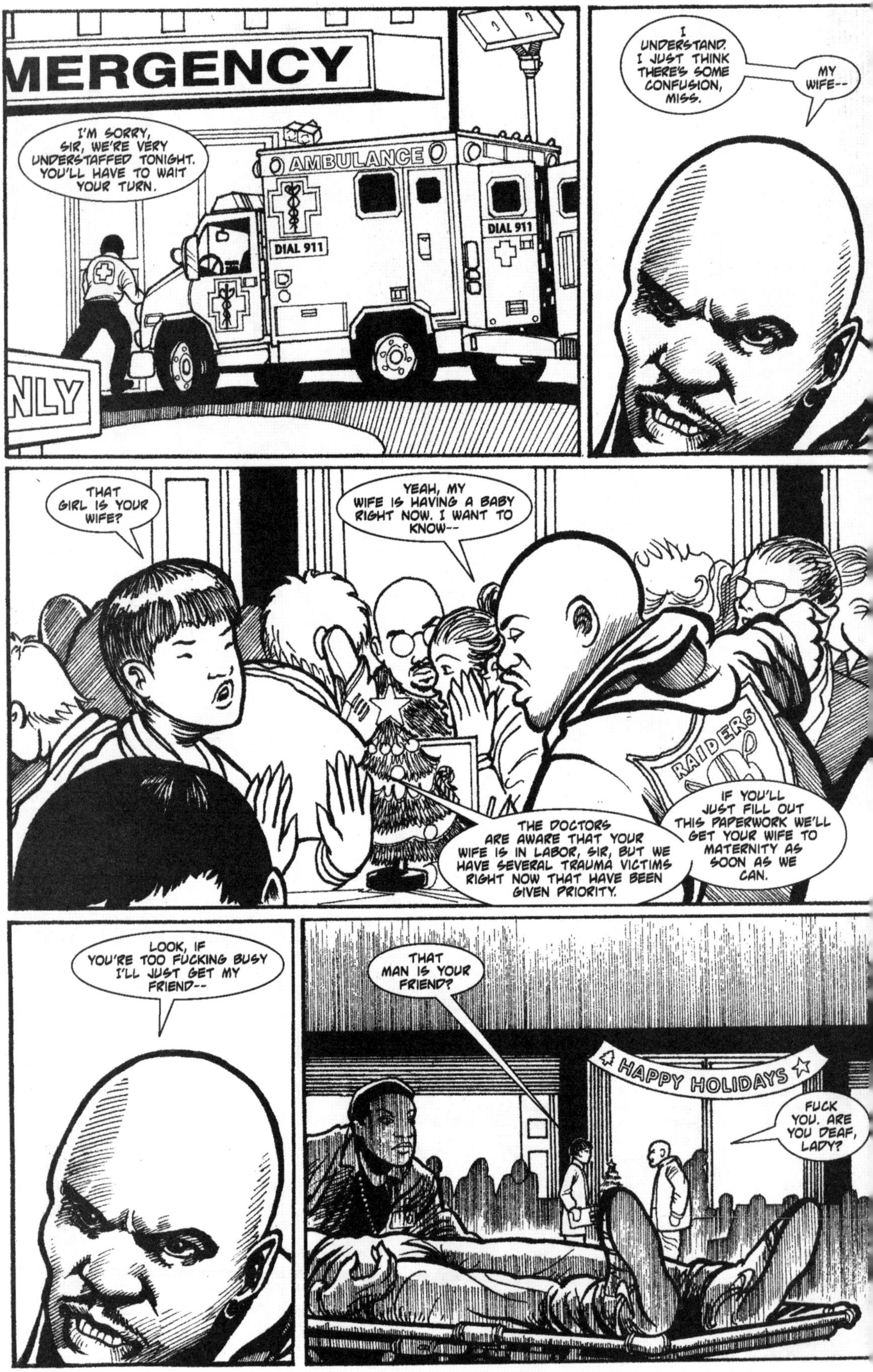
MERGENCY
AMBULANCE
DIAL 911
DIAL 911
NLY
I'M SORRY, SIR, WE'RE VERY UNDERSTAFFED TONIGHT. YOU'LL HAVE TO WAIT YOUR TURN.
I UNDERSTAND. I JUST THINK THERE'S SOME CONFUSION, MISS.
MY WIFE--
THAT GIRL IS YOUR WIFE?
YEAH, MY WIFE IS HAVING A BABY RIGHT NOW. I WANT TO KNOW--
RAIDERS
THE DOCTORS ARE AWARE THAT YOUR WIFE IS IN LABOR, SIR, BUT WE HAVE SEVERAL TRAUMA VICTIMS RIGHT NOW THAT HAVE BEEN GIVEN PRIORITY.
IF YOU'LL JUST FILL OUT THIS PAPERWORK WE'LL GET YOUR WIFE TO MATERNITY AS SOON AS WE CAN.
LOOK, IF YOU'RE TOO FUCKING BUSY I'LL JUST GET MY FRIEND--
THAT MAN IS YOUR FRIEND?
HAPPY HOLIDAYS
FUCK YOU. ARE YOU DEAF, LADY?

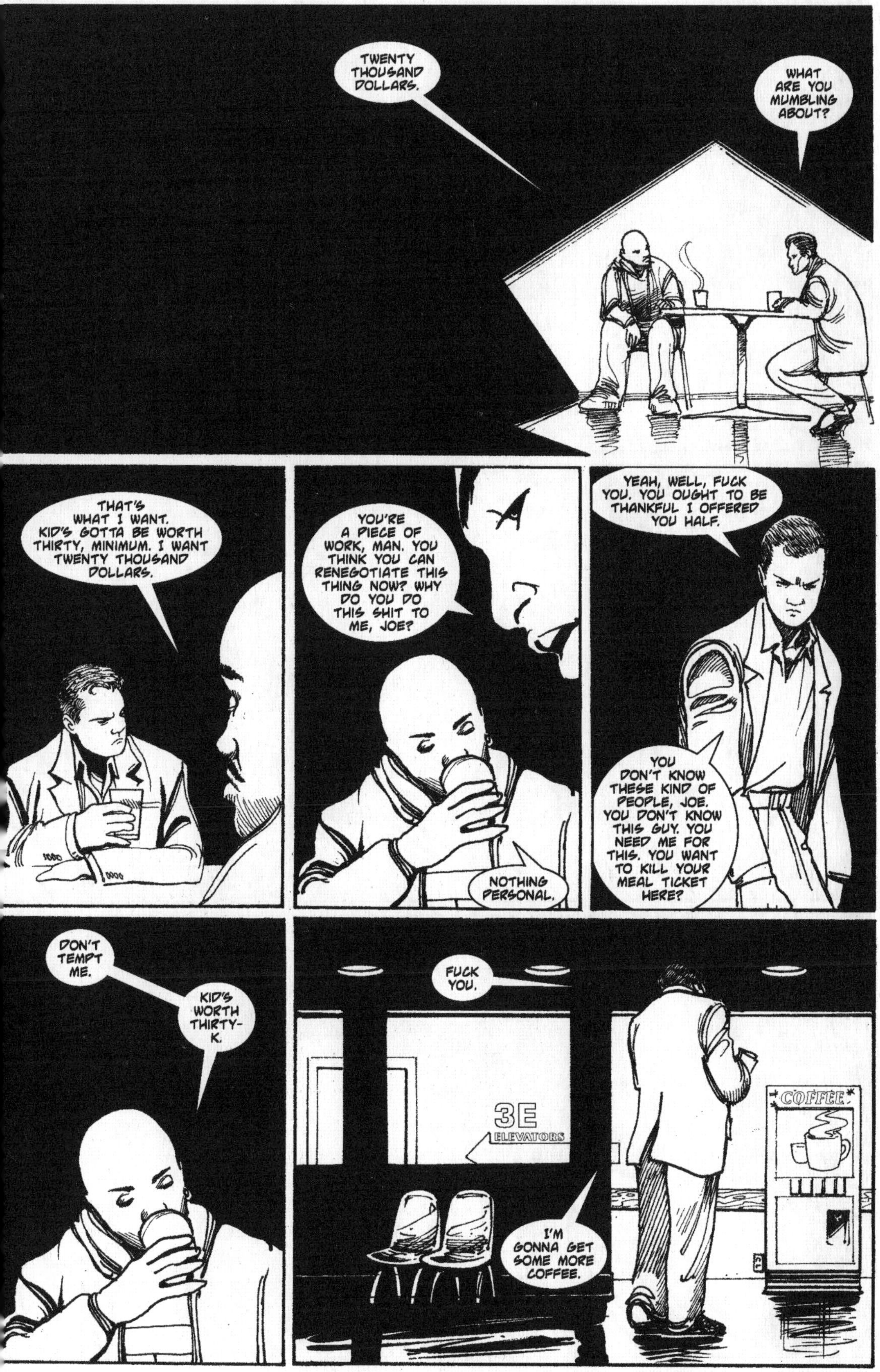
TWENTY THOUSAND DOLLARS.
WHAT ARE YOU MUMBLING ABOUT?
THAT'S WHAT I WANT. KID'S GOTTA BE WORTH THIRTY, MINIMUM. I WANT TWENTY THOUSAND DOLLARS.
YOU'RE A PIECE OF WORK, MAN. YOU THINK YOU CAN RENEGOTIATE THIS THING NOW? WHY DO YOU DO THIS SHIT TO ME, JOE?
NOTHING PERSONAL.
YEAH, WELL, FUCK YOU. YOU OUGHT TO BE THANKFUL I OFFERED YOU HALF.
YOU DON'T KNOW THESE KIND OF PEOPLE, JOE. YOU DON'T KNOW THIS GUY. YOU NEED ME FOR THIS. YOU WANT TO KILL YOUR MEAL TICKET HERE?
DON'T TEMPT ME.
KID'S WORTH THIRTY-K.
FUCK YOU.
3E
ELEVATORS
COFFEE
I'M GONNA GET SOME MORE COFFEE.

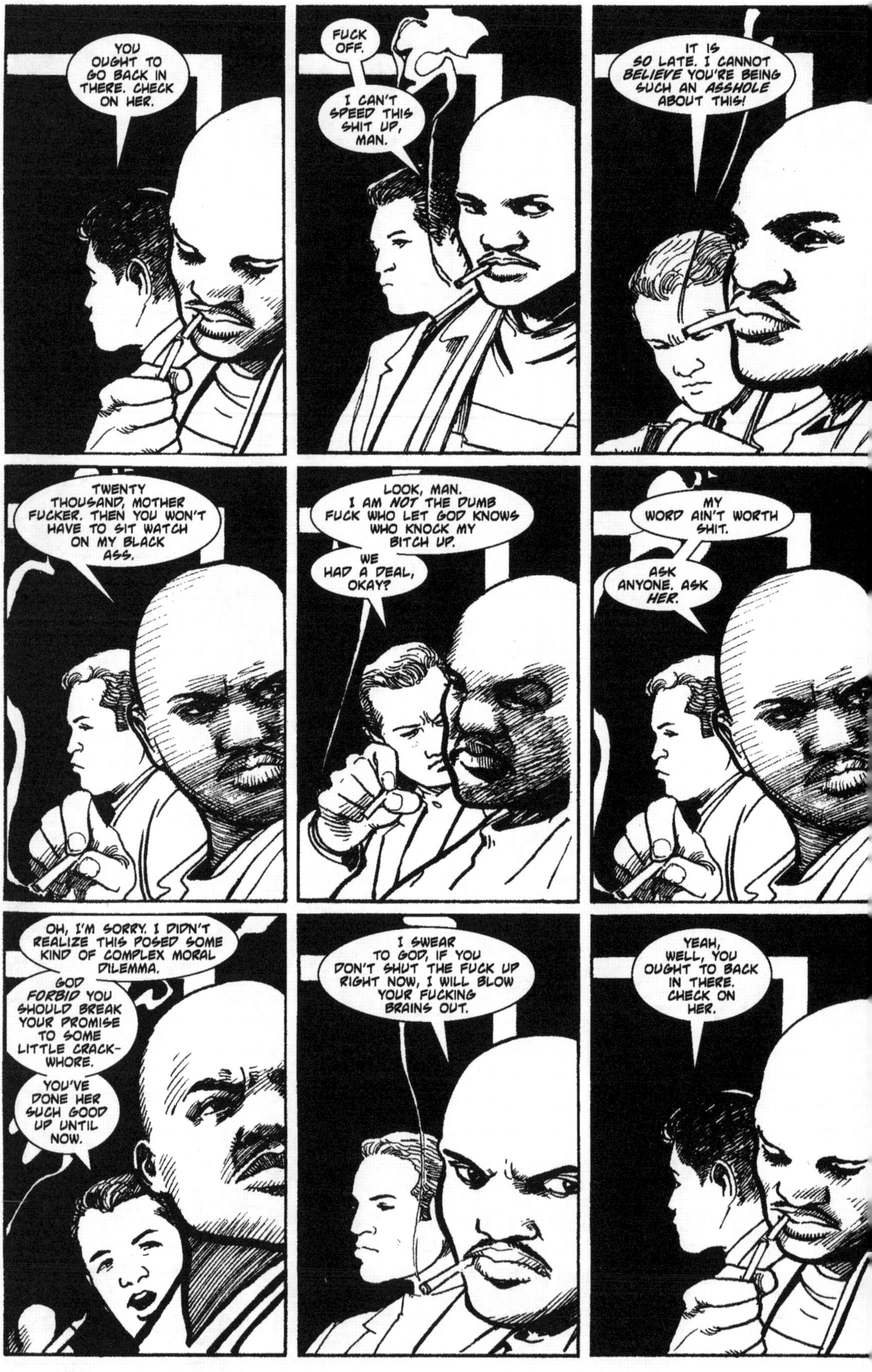
YOU OUGHT TO GO BACK IN THERE. CHECK ON HER.
FUCK OFF.
I CAN'T SPEED THIS SHIT UP, MAN.
IT IS SO LATE. I CANNOT BELIEVE YOU'RE BEING SUCH AN ASSHOLE ABOUT THIS!
TWENTY THOUSAND, MOTHER FUCKER. THEN YOU WON'T HAVE TO SIT WATCH ON MY BLACK ASS.
LOOK, MAN. I AM NOT THE DUMB FUCK WHO LET GOD KNOWS WHO KNOCK MY BITCH UP.
WE HAD A DEAL, OKAY?
MY WORD AIN'T WORTH SHIT.
ASK ANYONE. ASK HER.
OH, I'M SORRY. I DIDN'T REALIZE THIS POSED SOME KIND OF COMPLEX MORAL DILEMMA.
GOD FORBID YOU SHOULD BREAK YOUR PROMISE TO SOME LITTLE CRACK-WHORE.
YOU'VE DONE HER SUCH GOOD UP UNTIL NOW.
I SWEAR TO GOD, IF YOU DON'T SHUT THE FUCK UP RIGHT NOW, I WILL BLOW YOUR FUCKING BRAINS OUT.
YEAH, WELL, YOU OUGHT TO BACK IN THERE. CHECK ON HER.

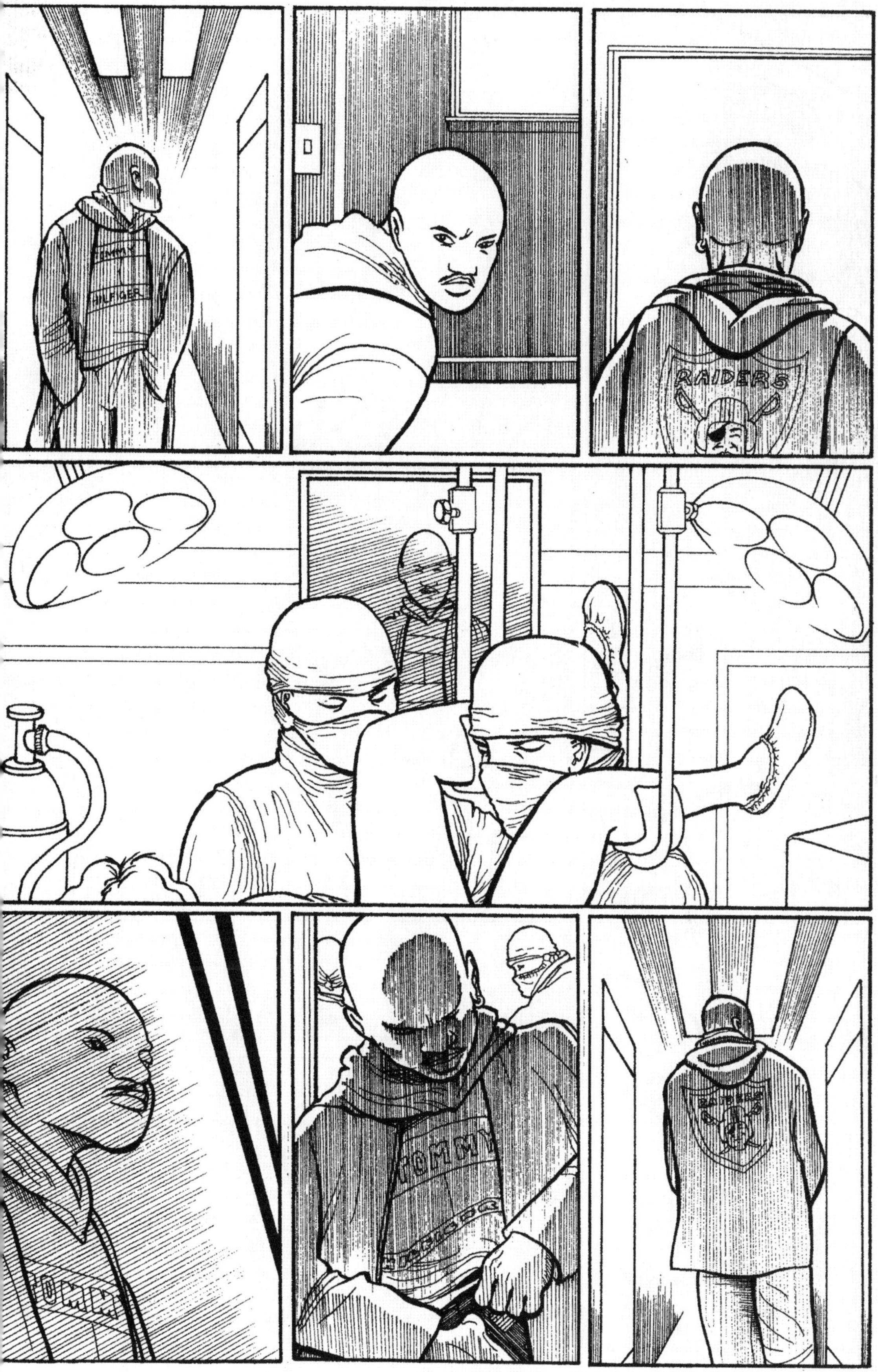
TOMMY
HILFIGER
RAIDERS
TOMMY

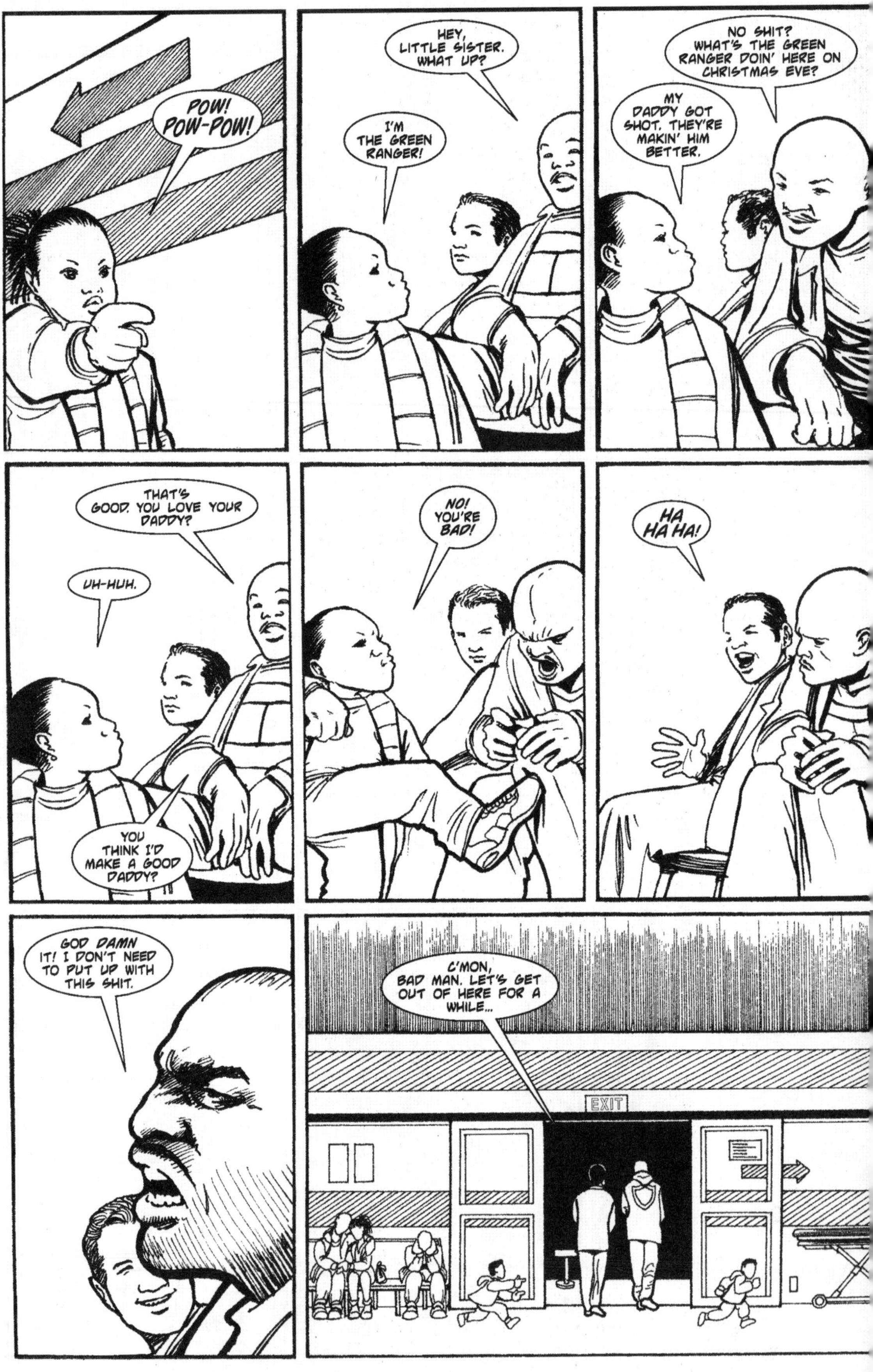
POW! POW-POW!
HEY, LITTLE SISTER. WHAT UP?
I'M THE GREEN RANGER!
NO SHIT? WHAT'S THE GREEN RANGER DOIN' HERE ON CHRISTMAS EVE?
MY DADDY GOT SHOT. THEY'RE MAKIN' HIM BETTER.
THAT'S GOOD. YOU LOVE YOUR DADDY?
UH-HUH.
YOU THINK I'D MAKE A GOOD DADDY?
NO! YOU'RE BAD!
HA HA HA!
GOD DAMN IT! I DON'T NEED TO PUT UP WITH THIS SHIT.
C'MON, BAD MAN. LET'S GET OUT OF HERE FOR A WHILE...
EXIT

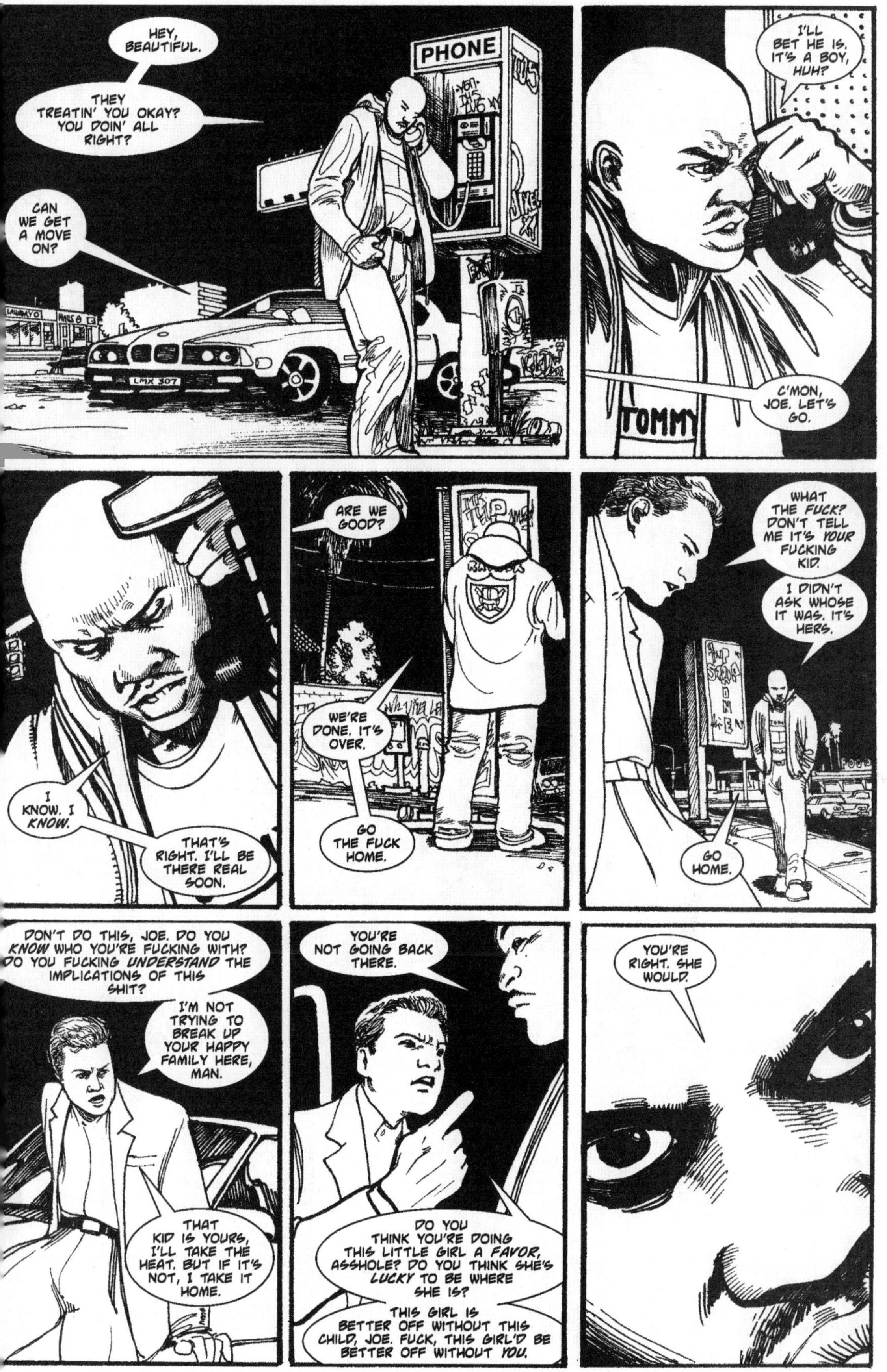
HEY, BEAUTIFUL.
THEY TREATIN' YOU OKAY? YOU DOIN' ALL RIGHT?
CAN WE GET A MOVE ON?
PHONE
LMX 307
I'LL BET HE IS. IT'S A BOY, HUH?
TOMMY
C'MON, JOE. LET'S GO.
I KNOW. I *KNOW.*
THAT'S RIGHT. I'LL BE THERE REAL SOON.
ARE WE GOOD?
WE'RE DONE. IT'S OVER.
GO THE FUCK HOME.
WHAT THE *FUCK?* DON'T TELL ME IT'S *YOUR* FUCKING KID.
I DIDN'T ASK WHOSE IT WAS. IT'S HERS.
GO HOME.
DON'T DO THIS, JOE. DO YOU *KNOW* WHO YOU'RE FUCKING WITH? DO YOU FUCKING *UNDERSTAND* THE IMPLICATIONS OF THIS SHIT?
I'M NOT TRYING TO BREAK UP YOUR HAPPY FAMILY HERE, MAN.
THAT KID IS YOURS, I'LL TAKE THE HEAT. BUT IF IT'S NOT, I TAKE IT HOME.
YOU'RE NOT GOING BACK THERE.
DO YOU THINK YOU'RE DOING THIS LITTLE GIRL A *FAVOR,* ASSHOLE? DO YOU THINK SHE'S *LUCKY* TO BE WHERE SHE IS?
THIS GIRL IS BETTER OFF WITHOUT THIS CHILD, JOE. FUCK, THIS GIRL'D BE BETTER OFF WITHOUT *YOU.*
YOU'RE RIGHT. SHE WOULD.

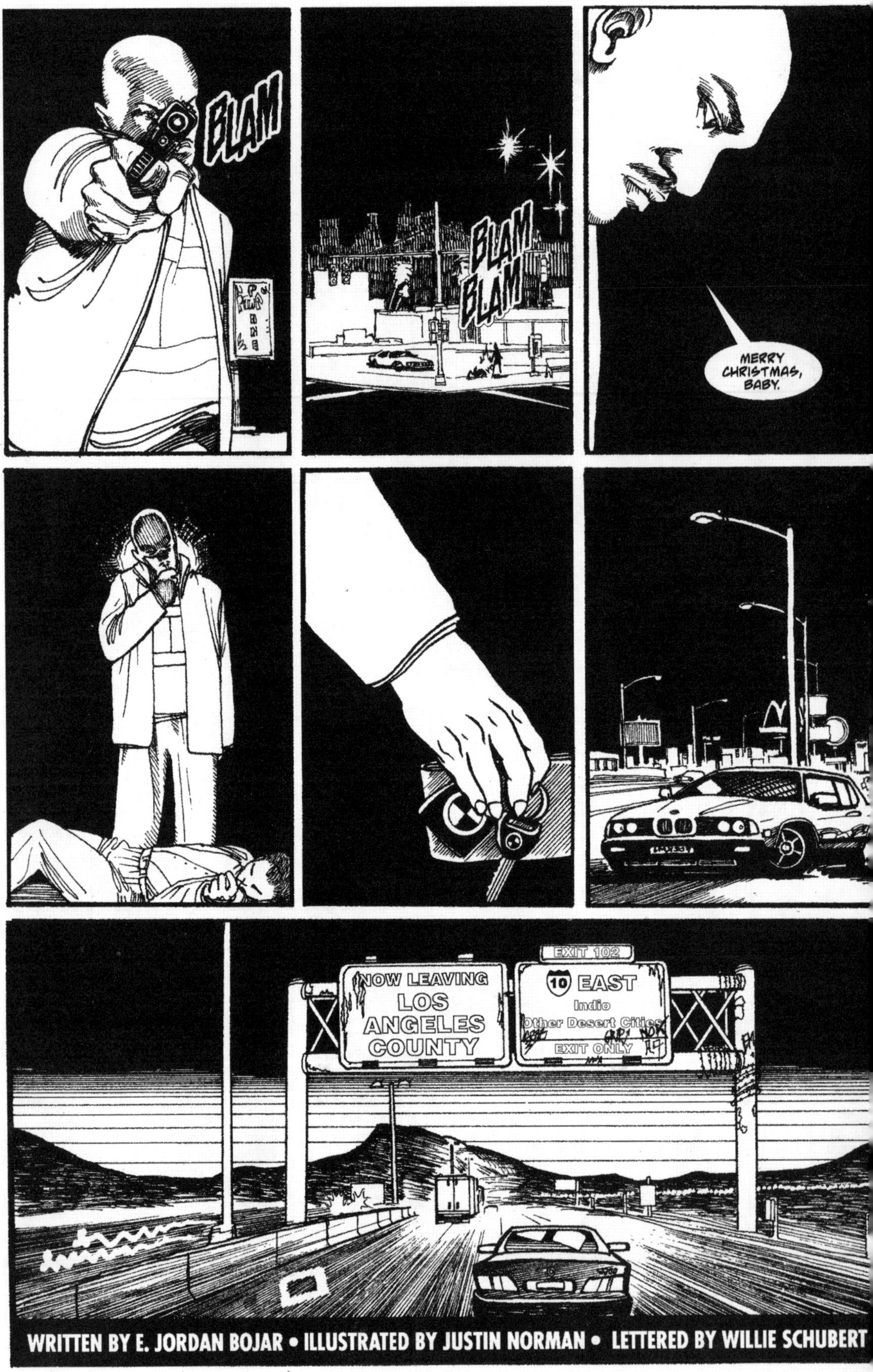

BLAM
BLAM
BLAM
MERRY CHRISTMAS, BABY.
EXIT 102
NOW LEAVING
LOS ANGELES COUNTY
10 EAST
Indio
Other Desert Cities
EXIT ONLY

WRITTEN BY E. JORDAN BOJAR • ILLUSTRATED BY JUSTIN NORMAN • LETTERED BY WILLIE SCHUBERT